OCCASIO

Anticipating Balance of Payments Crises

The Role of Early Warning Systems

Andrew Berg, Eduardo Borensztein,
Gian Maria Milesi-Ferretti, and Catherine Pattillo

INTERNATIONAL MONETARY FUND
Washington DC
1999

Production: IMF Graphics Section
Typesetting: Jack Federici
Figures: In-Ok Yoon

Cataloging-in-Publication Data

Anticipating balance of payments crises : the role of early warning systems /
  Andrew Berg . . . [et al.]— Washington D.C. International Monetary
  Fund, 1999.
      p.   cm. — (Occasional paper, ISSN 0251-6365 ; no. 186)
    Includes bibliographical references.
    ISBN 1-55775-828-X
  1. Balance of payments – Developing countries.   2. Balance of pay-
ments.   3. Currency question.   4. Financial crises I. Berg, Andrew.   II
Occasional paper (International Monetary Fund) ; no. 186.

HG3890.A57 1999

Price: US$18.00
(US$15.00 to full-time faculty members and
students at universities and colleges)

Please send orders to:
International Monetary Fund, Publication Services
700 19th Street, N.W., Washington, D.C. 20431, U.S.A.
Tel.: (202) 623-7430   Telefax: (202) 623-7201
E-mail: publications@imf.org
Internet: http://www.imf.org

recycled paper

Contents

Preface

The material presented in this paper was originally prepared for discussions in the IMF Executive Board in January 1999. The authors are especially indebted to Paul R. Masson for his overall guidance and helpful suggestions on the various drafts. The paper, or material incorporated in it, has benefited from the comments of members of the Executive Board and staff in the Research Department as well as other departments of the IMF. In this connection the authors are particularly grateful to Stanley Fischer, Michael Mussa, Peter Clark, Enrica Detragiache, Ricardo Faini, Robert Flood, and Christian Mulder.

The authors would like to express thanks to a number of commentators in the academic and policy community, notably Graciela Kaminsky, Carmen Reinhart, Andrew Rose, and Aaron Tornell for help in reproducing and interpreting their results and Hali Edison, Robert Hodrick, and Steve Kamin for comments.

The authors would also like to thank Manzoor Gill and Nada Mora for superb research assistance, and Usha David and Margaret Dapaah for excellent secretarial assistance. Esha Ray of the External Relations Department edited and coordinated the production of the paper.

The views expressed here, as well as any errors, are solely the responsibility of the authors and do not necessarily reflect the opinions of the IMF or its Executive Directors.

I Overview

Recent years have witnessed an increase in the frequency of currency and balance of payments crises in developing countries. More important, the crises have become more virulent, have caused widespread disruption to other developing countries, and have even had repercussions on advanced economies. In some cases, the crises have also been quite unexpected and have affected countries with strong economic performance. Even when economies were perceived as more vulnerable to crises, the timing of speculative attacks has often caught observers and policymakers by surprise. This course of events, in part related to the increased volume and volatility of private international financial flows, has stimulated research on the prediction of balance of payments crises.[1]

Clearly it would be desirable to have a system for identifying looming crises so that steps could be taken to avoid them. With the increasing liberalization of capital movements and the globalization of financial markets, unsustainable policies may at times be disciplined by an early reaction of financial markets, while on other occasions, they may be exacerbated by strong capital inflows that are later reversed as investor sentiment suddenly changes. The resulting crisis may itself be associated with economic disruption and welfare losses that go beyond those justified by the economic fundamentals, making crisis prediction and prevention an important objective. This paper aims to assess the progress of attempts to develop systematic empirical frameworks for predicting balance of payments crises.

A number of projects were initiated after the Mexican crisis of December 1994 to design an early warning system (EWS).[2] These efforts have multiplied since the onset of the Asian crisis.[3] Early warning systems apply some statistical method to predict the likelihood that a country will face a currency or balance of payments crisis, defined in a precise way, over a given time horizon.[4] Their frameworks focus on economic and financial variables that are likely to provide an early indication of a vulnerable balance of payments position or unsustainable exchange rate level. These variables typically include indicators of domestic macroeconomic imbalances and banking sector weakness, such as fiscal deficits and domestic credit growth; overvaluation of the exchange rate, such as measures of relative prices or costs, the current account deficit, and export growth; and of external vulnerability and contagion, such as external liabilities relative to international reserves and the incidence of crises in other countries. In sum, the range of possible variables encompasses both the fundamentals of the domestic economy and the vulnerability to changes in market sentiment and the global environment.

To predict crises, their causes must be clearly understood. Two competing strands of theories—called first- and second-generation models—are reviewed in this paper (Section II). The first focuses on the consequences of such policies as excessive credit growth in provoking a depletion of foreign exchange reserves and making a devaluation inevitable. The second emphasizes the trade-offs between internal and external balance that the policymaker faces in defending a peg: if the costs in terms of unemployment or financial sector fragility of using interest

---

[1]A currency crisis usually refers to a situation in which speculative attacks force a sharp devaluation. A balance of payments crisis is a broader concept that involves a shortage of reserves to cover balance of payments needs. This paper focuses on balance of payments crises as well as currency crises. Empirically, this means that the paper considers situations in which speculative attacks force a sharp drop in international reserves or a sharp devaluation or both. Furthermore, although most of the theoretical literature concentrates on attacks against a pegged exchange rate regime, this paper takes a broader view, considering also the possibility of speculative attacks against more flexible regimes, such as managed floats.

[2]Most notably, Kaminsky, Lizondo, and Reinhart (1998). More detailed references are provided in Sections III and IV.

[3]The staff at a number of institutions, including the Federal Reserve Board, the Federal Reserve Bank of New York, and the Bank for International Settlements are also undertaking research in the area of early warning systems to complement their analysis of financial markets.

[4]While all models try to anticipate exchange rate movements, some of them take a broader focus and try to anticipate both currency crashes and failed attacks. The latter are evidenced by losses in international reserves and/or sharp increases in domestic interest rates.

rates to defend the exchange rate are too high, the authorities may choose to devalue. The endogeneity of the policy choice, together with the fact that expectations affect the trade-off faced by the government, raise the possibility that crises may be self-fulfilling. For example, investors who expect a devaluation may, by raising the cost of servicing outstanding debt, make a crisis more likely. Crises are likely to be more difficult to predict in this latter case, since they depend in part on investor sentiment. Finally, there is some evidence that crises may also be triggered by contagion effects.

Ideally, an early warning system should try to identify situations that pose a distinct risk of a crisis affecting the external payments of a country or a large devaluation of its currency. But what are the events or situations that a system should provide warnings about? In some cases, such as the abandonment of a peg, a collapse in the value of the domestic currency, or a default in international payments, there is no ambiguity in identifying the event. But should the definition also include cases that involve sizable but unsuccessful currency attacks, such as Argentina in 1995 or Brazil in 1997? It would seem apparent that the economic authorities should be alert to any situation in which the external position is vulnerable; this also includes currency attacks that ultimately result in "close calls" but no devaluation. In fact, whether an attack ends in a currency crisis or not may well depend on the resolve of the government in defending its currency, on accompanying policy measures, and on the availability of external financing rather than on the conditions that originated the attack. Adopting this broader definition of crisis may make the problem of prediction more difficult, to the extent that failed attacks are truly different from currency collapses, but the broader measure will be more useful to policymakers. The paper discusses the specific empirical implementation of alternative crisis definitions (Section III).

How well have existing early warning systems done in predicting currency or balance of payments crises? Section IV examines the performance of three representative frameworks (plus an extension developed in the paper). The short answer is, they have had mixed success. The predictions from the most promising models contain substantial information about the risks of crisis, but they often provide false alarms. A representative model produces a warning signal (indication that a crisis is approaching) in about 50 percent of the cases in which it should have signaled because a crisis did indeed happen at some point over the following two years. This means, in a typical case, that during the two years before a crisis the model issued a warning signal on about 12 of the 24 months. But the warnings issued by the typical early warning system model are not very reliable. About 60 percent of the times that the typical model issued a warning, no crisis occurred during the following two years.

Some care should be taken in interpreting false alarms as "mistakes" made by the models. First, the authorities in these countries may have taken policy measures to ward off a looming crisis. More generally, it may be that these false alarms occurred in situations in which countries were truly at risk but did not suffer a crisis because of favorable external developments or even good luck. As discussed in Section II, theoretical models that emphasize self-fulfilling crises imply that, for a range of values of fundamentals, crises may happen but are not inevitable. The best an early warning system could do would be to assign higher probabilities of crisis to countries that are more vulnerable to a shift in expectations. This would still be useful information, as the model would essentially generate correct warnings, even though many of these warnings would be counted as false alarms.

Models tend to perform much more reliably for the historical period for which they were designed and estimated ("in sample") than for later periods ("out of sample"). This is particularly true when the out-of-sample period considered is one that took place after the research was conducted, and thus could not have been, implicitly or explicitly, incorporated into the design of the system. For example, Section IV studies the performance in relation to the Asian crisis of three representative models that were designed and estimated before 1997, in addition to another one developed after the Asian crisis. In the former three cases, the researchers did not know about the factors present in the unfolding of the Asian crisis, so that those events did not affect their choice of variables or any other aspect of the specification of the model. Applying this more stringent test, the out-of-sample and out-of-researcher-awareness period, the models examined do indeed tend to perform somewhat more poorly. The most successful model suffers some degradation in performance out of sample. The number of correct warning signals during the two years prior to the crises of 1997 drops to about 34 percent. However, the number of false alarms (when the model indicated that a crisis was approaching but no crisis took place during the following two years) also drops to about 51 percent.

Although it is possible, in principle, to calibrate models to forecast a larger fraction of the emerging crises, this would imply a cost in terms of the reliability of the signals. That is, the number of false alarms—predicted crises that do not materialize—rises as the number of missed crises falls. The precise calibration of the early warning systems thus depends on the relative cost associated with each type of error. In principle, since the purpose of such a system is to anticipate currency crises, one would prefer a specification that is fairly sensitive to symptoms and would not fail to issue warnings very often when a crisis is indeed approaching. But one should be aware that, in such cases, even the best-performing model is bound to produce its share of false signals—currency attacks, and even currency collapses—that are predicted by the model but will fail to materialize.

What is the standard against which to judge the value of forecasts generated by an early warning system? Available measures of expectations by market participants display a poor record with respect to recent events in anticipating crises. For example, a direct measure of exchange rate expectations from the surveys carried out by the Financial Times Currency Forecaster (which surveys banks, multinational companies, and professional forecasters on a monthly basis) suggests that markets had little inkling of the approaching crises in Mexico in 1994, or in Thailand in 1997 (Figure 1).[5] The 30-day-ahead exchange rate forecast showed virtually no increase in expectations of a devaluation in the months just before the currency collapsed nor did the 12-month forecast. In fact, in the case of Mexico, the 12-month-ahead expectations turned more pessimistic in the second half of 1995 and in 1996, when Mexico was actually already emerging from the crisis. In the Asian crisis, countries' expectations of exchange rate depreciation went up sharply in October 1997, when markets in Hong Kong Special Administrative Region (SAR) and throughout the region displayed significant turbulence, but abated in November 1997, just before the collapse of the Korean won and the renewed weakness of some other currencies in the region.

Market expectations as embedded in asset prices also have not provided clear signals in recent episodes. Interest differentials (the spread between domestic and foreign interest rates, themselves a function of monetary policy and other factors as well) did not widen significantly prior to the Mexican crisis.[6] Spreads on Brady bonds and Eurobonds, instead of providing an early signal of worsening of confidence, appear to have widened only at the time

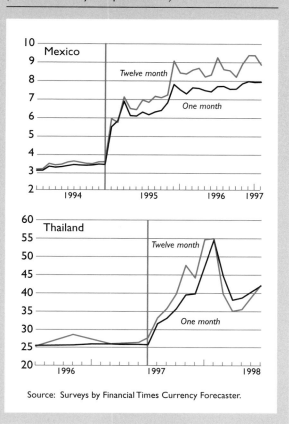

Figure 1. Exchange Rate Expectations
(In national currency units per U.S. dollar)

Source: Surveys by Financial Times Currency Forecaster.

currency pressures were already well under way. In the Asian crisis, spreads hardly increased in the months prior to the flotation of the baht, and rose only in late October 1997, four full months after the event.[7]

This suggests that, although early warning systems are hardly infallible, they can contribute to the analysis of external risks in emerging countries (Section V). While they look at many of the same economic and financial variables that most analysts do, their strength is that they process the information contained in the rather large number of relevant variables in a systematic way that maximizes their ability to predict currency and balance of payments crises, based on the historical experience of a large number of countries. Often an early warning system can translate this infor-

---

[5]The figure is from Goldfajn and Valdés (1999), where a more systematic analysis of exchange rate expectations is conducted. See also Agénor and Masson (1999).

[6]While it is possible that an increase in the expected devaluation was offset by other factors, in particular the change in the composition of Mexican debt toward dollar-indexed securities (Werner, 1996), there was not an unequivocal signal of higher expected depreciation that could be picked up from interest differentials.

[7]Actions by rating agencies such as Moody's and Standard and Poor's have also not provided reliable leading indicators, as in the case of the recent Asian currency crises (Adams, Mathieson, Schinasi, and Chadha, 1998, Box 2.13).

mation into a composite measure of vulnerability. Being based on a well-defined methodology, it is less likely to be clouded by preconceptions about the expected economic performance of particular countries.

Furthermore, an early warning system can be a useful tool to rank the relative vulnerability of a group of countries, which is more difficult to assess on the basis of a country-by-country analysis.

II What Causes Balance of Payments Crises?

The sudden collapse of exchange rate pegs in the absence of an immediate major change in economic fundamentals can seem a clear proof of irrationality in foreign exchange markets. An important contribution of the academic literature on this topic was to dispel that notion, showing that a sudden run on foreign exchange reserves that forces the abandonment of a peg can be, for example, the natural outcome of an inconsistency between monetary and exchange rate policy or the rational response by investors to a shift in expectations regarding macroeconomic policies. The Appendix provides a selective review of the causes of currency crises that have been identified in the, by now extensive, theoretical literature. This section examines the features of the main crisis episodes over the past 20 years and what they suggest about the origins and symptoms of approaching crises.

Different Episodes, Different Determinants?

The survey of the literature on currency crises in the Appendix suggests the distinction between crises that are caused by a deterioration in fundamentals and those that result from self-fulfilling speculative attacks. But even for the latter, it is often the case that some weakness in the fundamentals of the economy makes the country vulnerable to the speculative attack and the authorities less inclined to defend an exchange rate parity. Thus, a critical step in designing an early warning system for balance of payments crises is to identify those weak or inconsistent fundamentals. The problem is that the relevant fundamentals may be different in each episode. They may reflect disequilibria in the trade account or in the capital account. They may respond to private sector imbalances or to public sector deficits. They may be related to shocks affecting the real sector of the economy or the financial sector. The challenge in designing a unified approach is then to take into account all the relevant factors that are potential indicators of approaching crises.

Indeed, the changes in global financial markets and in emerging market economies have had an im-

portant effect on the genesis of crises. In "traditional" (first generation) balance of payments crises the fundamental disequilibrium typically involves some macroeconomic imbalance, such as a fiscal deficit financed through money creation that at some point becomes incompatible with an exchange rate peg. By contrast, in "modern" balance of payments crises issues such as self-fulfilling speculative attacks, contagion, and weaknesses in domestic financial markets appear to be the most relevant proximate causes, in the context of less restricted capital movements. Naturally, the two types of determinants of crises are not mutually exclusive, and indeed, in some of the recent crises the traditional macroeconomic imbalances were clearly perceptible. But it is obvious that the development and globalization of financial markets have had a major impact on the nature of currency attacks and balance of payments crises.

A look at the major international crises of the past two decades exemplifies the evolution in the pattern of crises. The debt crisis of the 1980s, which started with the suspension of payments by Mexico in August 1982 and continued for almost a decade, reflected a mix of external shocks and domestic macroeconomic imbalances that had developed behind the screen of the strong capital inflows of the previous years. Most observers identified the reasons for the debt crisis as a combination of negative external shocks—such as a deterioration in the terms of trade, the sharp rise in U.S. dollar interest rates, and the global economic slowdown—and the internal macroeconomic imbalances that affected many of the debtor countries—such as fiscal deficits and currency overvaluation. To these factors, Dornbusch, Goldfajn, and Valdés (1995) add the mismanagement of capital inflows, especially through the provision of implicit or explicit exchange rate guarantees to private and state enterprise borrowers, in the context of pegged or predetermined exchange rates. The data in Table 1 are indicative of the unfavorable shift in external and internal fundamentals in the period immediately preceding the debt crisis.

It is therefore not surprising that most observers drawing lessons from the debt crisis of the 1980s re-

Table 1. Fifteen Heavily Indebted Countries: Summary Indicators[1]

	Average 1977–80	1981	1982	1983
Terms of trade (1977 = 100)	100	103	83	85
U.S. interest rate (federal funds rate, in percent)	9.5	16.4	12.3	9.1
Real exchange rate (1977 = 100)	109	129	107	98
Fiscal deficit (in percent of GDP)	2.9	5.6	6.6	6.1
GDP growth	4.8	0.4	0.5	−2.6

Source: International Monetary Fund, *International Financial Statistics.*

[1]The 15 countries are Argentina, Bolivia, Brazil, Chile, Colombia, Côte d'Ivoire, Ecuador, Mexico, Morocco, Nigeria, Peru, the Philippines, Uruguay, Venezuela, and Yugoslavia.

ferred to the need for appropriate domestic macroeconomic policies and structural reforms that would make economies more resilient to external shocks. For example, in his postmortem of the debt crisis, Cline (1995) emphasizes two policy prescriptions: to launch far-reaching structural reforms (especially trade liberalization and privatization) and to pursue sound macroeconomic policies (especially with reference to fiscal deficits but also keeping an eye on current account deficits that were the counterpart of excessive spending by the private sector).[8] It is noteworthy that problems related to domestic banking systems did not receive a prominent place in the analyses of the debt crisis of the 1980s. While some debtor countries, particularly in the Southern Cone, suffered severe banking crises, the reasons were generally interpreted as having to do with the aftermath of the external crisis in poorly regulated banking systems. That is, problems in the banking systems were not viewed as one of the deficiencies that had caused the external debt defaults.[9]

The Mexican crisis of 1994/95 suggested different explanations and different fundamentals. In this case, many observers pointed to self-fulfilling prophecies by market participants as being largely responsible for the collapse of the peso. But it was also recognized that an underlying vulnerability in the economy made the speculative attacks possible. In Mexico, large current account deficits (which resulted from an overvalued currency after a difficult inflation stabilization process) as well as the debt management policy followed just before the crisis had caused the accumulation of sizable short-term U.S. dollar-denominated debt; furthermore, the rapid expansion in the domestic financial sector had created a situation of poor quality loan portfolios and heavy exposure to an exchange rate devaluation. Calvo and Mendoza (1996) present two measures to summarize the vulnerability of the peso to a speculative attack. They are the adequacy of international reserves relative to M2 (which measures domestic liabilities of both the central bank and the banking system) and the adequacy of international reserves relative to the external short-term debt (both of the government and the private sector). As can be seen in Figure 2 the gap between international reserves and both types of liabilities widened significantly prior to the peso crisis.

Once again, economists, policymakers, and market participants made an effort to draw conclusions as to the reasons for the crisis and the best course to prevent recurrences. Summers (1995) presented ten lessons to be learned from the Mexican crisis, which differed in some significant ways from the conclusions that had been drawn after the debt crisis. Al-

---

[8]Other prescriptions had to do with the nature of the relationships between countries and their creditor banks: to favor market-based options for debt renegotiations and to avoid a socialization of private debts at time of distress.

[9]An exception may be Diaz-Alejandro (1985) with reference to Chile.

Figure 2. Mexico, 1994: Indicators of Vulnerability
(In billions of U.S. dollars)

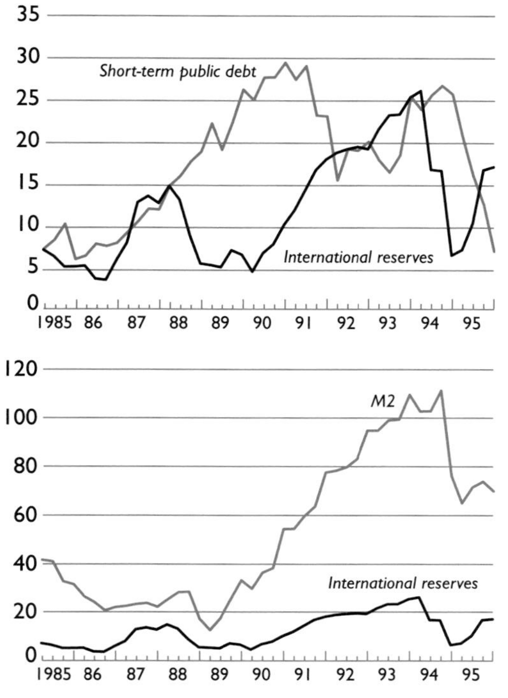

Sources: IMF, *International Financial Statistics*; and Bank of Mexico.

low for a number of years.[10] With the exception of Thailand, real exchange rates had not displayed any significant appreciation in the years leading to the crises, and although a slowdown in export growth had been recorded in some of the economies of the region since 1996, it had come after several years of very strong expansion. The loan portfolios of financial institutions, by contrast, had deteriorated significantly, and the corporate sector was excessively indebted and financially fragile, which resulted from years of poor lending and investment decisions. Indeed, weaknesses in the financial and corporate sectors seem to be the only common thread among all the affected countries in the region[11] though of course other countries also share those same problems.

There is a strong presumption that contagion, somehow defined, also played a major role, to the degree that some of the affected economies might not have had a crisis at all were it not for the negative market reaction triggered by Thailand. Although contagion had been strong after the 1994 Mexican crisis (the "tequila" effect), Latin American countries were mostly able to preserve currency stability, though certainly not without costs. Spillovers originating in financial markets, as well as herding behavior by investors (not only in terms of joining in the stampede out of a currency but also in their propensity to flee from other countries in the same region), appear to have played an important role in the Asian "contagion," in addition to more traditional channels related to trade.

Searching for Common Symptoms

Even if the ultimate causes of balance of payments crises may differ to some extent from case to case, it might be possible to identify a common pattern in the development of crises that becomes detectable as the process starts to unfold. For example, international reserves may become dangerously low at some point in the development of a currency crisis, or the level of external debt commitments may become too high relative to the relevant available resources. Alternatively, movements in asset prices may also follow a common pattern in anticipation of currency crises. For example, as markets identify a number of perhaps subtle signs of distress, this

though the soundness and sustainability of domestic policies still figure at the top of the list, the new emphasis is on ways to deal with volatile financial markets, such as increasing transparency in economic data and creating new mechanisms to provide rapid financial support by the international community. Another recommendation is to maintain the current account balance within moderate bounds (deficits not exceeding 5 percent of GDP) to reduce vulnerability to speculative attacks, which is heightened when the deficits are financed by short-term debt or other easily reversible financial instruments. Again, it is interesting to note that banking sector problems were not mentioned in Summers's analysis, despite their noticeable role in the unfolding of the Mexican crisis.

The Asian crisis put financial markets in the forefront of attention. In the affected Asian countries, traditional sources of fundamental imbalances were largely absent. The fiscal position was quite robust for all countries, and inflation had been moderate or

---

[10]But the fiscal situation would have been considered less favorably if allowance was made for the contingent liability of the government arising from the support to financial institutions that might become necessary. But even making such allowance, the fiscal position would not have suggested an unsustainable burden.

[11]See Krugman (1998); Kochhar, Loungani, and Stone (1998); Berg (1999); and Radelet and Sachs (1998b).

would be reflected in asset prices, such as increased risk premiums on the vulnerable currencies.

It should be evident that the vulnerability of an economy to a balance of payments crisis increases significantly when the level of international reserves is inadequate. While excessively low reserves must be the most universal sign of an approaching crisis, determining what constitutes an adequate level of reserves in particular cases is difficult. In principle, the relevant comparator should be the level of liabilities that may imply claims on reserves. The level of liquid monetary assets (say, M2) is a natural measure of potential demand for foreign assets from domestic sources. Even if the currency is not fully convertible or purchases of foreign exchange are severely restricted, the money supply could fuel the demand for foreign exchange through parallel markets or some indirect external transactions. To the extent that flight by external creditors is likely to be at the heart of the crisis, the volume of foreign debt payments coming due in the short term is an appropriate yardstick to judge whether the level of reserves is adequate. In other cases, the relevant comparison for the level of reserves would be domestic debt payments coming due, as these may become a source of capital outflows (such as Tesobonos in Mexico or GKOs in Russia). In fact, with both domestic and foreign investors holding the "domestic" debt (bonds issued in the domestic markets) and with part of the domestic debt sometimes denominated in foreign currency or linked to the exchange rate, the distinction between domestic and foreign debt becomes blurred.[12]

It is clear, however, that indicators such as those above are not meaningful if they are not considered in conjunction with "fundamentals," that is, the external balance position and the domestic macroeconomic situation of the country. Furthermore, the level of vulnerability implied by a given international reserves coverage would vary at times when investors display a generally more or less favorable sentiment toward emerging economies, or a higher or lower propensity toward contagion. For example, a country may have a large volume of payments coming due in a given year for purely coincidental reasons, but this would not be a meaningful indicator of vulnerability if the country displays strong fundamentals and the mood in international financial markets is favorable to emerging markets. Conversely, a relatively high level of international reserves could be short-lived in the presence of large deficits and negative investor sentiment.

Another relevant set of symptoms may be found in international financial markets themselves. After controlling for other factors, the evolution of prices in financial markets may provide indications of increased risk. The expectation of a devaluation of the domestic currency, for example, would widen interest differentials between assets denominated in domestic and foreign currencies. If economic difficulties are envisioned, investors would also pull out of sovereign debt instruments, and possibly the domestic stock markets, and this would be reflected in widening spreads on instruments such as Brady bonds and declining equity prices. Yet these different asset prices may provide apparently conflicting signals, because they are affected by different risks. For example, Brady bond spreads reflect the risk of default by the country on those bond payments. This risk is related to the risk of a currency collapse, as a balance of payments crisis may trigger both, but it is conceivable that in other situations the two risks may not be perceived as concomitant. For example, the exchange rate of a country may be considered to be overvalued and likely to be significantly devalued but the servicing of foreign bonds may be considered safe. In fact, in the Mexican and Asian crises it appeared that the risk of nonpayment on external bonds of the affected countries—as perceived by markets—rose *after* rather than before the currency devaluations.

In sum, the economic literature and the analysis of the broad trends in the major currency crises of the past years suggest a general strategy for the identification of the variables that may play an important role in the design of an early warning system. First, an early warning system should consider the evolution of economic fundamentals. The role of economic fundamentals is of prime importance both in the "traditional" (or first-generation) balance of payments crises and in the "modern" (or second-generation) crises. The former focuses on inconsistencies between the policy stance and the exchange rate, while the latter acknowledges that some weakness in the fundamentals is required for a currency attack to persuade the government to abandon the defense of the currency. It is true, however, that the range of fundamentals that are relevant has broadened with the changes in international financial markets. In particular, signals of stress in the banking sector should receive more attention and should be considered along with more traditional fundamentals such as those related to the external position of the economy, including the level of the real exchange rate or the current account balance, and those describing the domestic macroeconomic situation, such as fiscal balances and credit growth.

Second, an early warning system should also consider indicators of the likelihood of a successful de-

---

[12]It is noteworthy that the reserves to imports ratio, the traditional measure of reserves adequacy has become obsolete for many emerging economies with large capital inflows and outflows.

fense of the currency in case of an attack, as a less vulnerable currency is not likely to suffer serious attacks. In particular, the coverage offered by the level of international reserves relative to possible short-run liabilities of external and domestic origin has been identified as a measure of the vulnerability of the domestic currency to an attack. These variables could be supplemented by other data, such as the forward position of the central bank and other official or private institutions, and available lines of credit or other contingency financing, although these data may be harder to obtain.

It is important to note that these two types of variables—fundamentals and vulnerability indicators—play essentially a complementary role. Countries with weak fundamentals but good liquidity would not stay in a strong position for long, and conversely, countries with relatively bad liquidity but sound fundamentals, while not immune to attacks from "uninformed" investors, are less likely to be attacked and more likely to be successful in defending an attack.

Finally, indicators of market sentiment may also have a role in an early warning system, for example, indicators that can be extracted from asset prices or from developments in other countries that may trigger contagion. Market sentiment is a powerful force but is difficult to measure, and related indicators may also be relatively uninformative because they tend to provide signals only very late in the gestation of a crisis. Yet it is obvious that any analyst should be watching signs of market sentiment and thus their incorporation in an early warning system deserves to be explored.

III Issues in the Design of Early Warning Systems

Much of the empirical work on currency crises has been aimed at characterizing the stylized facts in periods leading up to crises (event studies) or testing particular models of crises. Event studies, which assess whether the behavior of particular variables is discernibly different in the months before a crisis from average behavior during tranquil periods,[13] are systematic methods for the important first stages of "looking at the data." A prominent example is International Monetary Fund (1998), which studies currency crises in 50 advanced and emerging market countries. Many other studies test different theoretical models of currency crisis, with either multiple- or single-country data. Early warning systems, in contrast, are not concerned with explanations of specific crises or tests of particular theories; instead, they focus on finding the best methods that can be used to forecast crisis probabilities. This study concentrates exclusively on cross-country analyses with focus on developing countries.

An early warning system consists of a precise definition of crisis and a mechanism for generating predictions, including a set of variables that may help predict crises and a systematic method to obtain a prediction from those variables. Different models have followed different approaches to address a number of conceptual and practical issues that arise concerning both the definition of crisis and the design of the method to predict a crisis. The most important issues concern the definition of crisis, the methodology to apply, and the choice of variables to serve as predictors.

What Are We Trying to Predict?

In the theoretical work discussed in Section II, currency crises are typically characterized by sudden attacks on a pegged exchange rate regime. A "failed" attack may result in reserve losses or higher interest rates but no devaluation, while a successful attack results in a step devaluation or a flotation and depreciation, perhaps after reserve losses and/or interest rate increases. In practice, exchange rate systems subject to speculative attack include not only pegs but also more-or-less managed floating exchange rates before the crisis. For example, a steep depreciation of a floating currency may also constitute a crisis. The need to systematically distinguish crises from other movements in exchange rates and reserves implies that translating the concept of speculative attacks into an empirical definition of crises is not straightforward.

Models that attempt to predict only successful attacks define a currency crisis as a sufficiently large change in the nominal or real exchange rate over a short period of time. For example, in their 1996 study, Frankel and Rose defined a currency crisis as a change in the nominal exchange rate of over 25 percent in one year, using annual average data. Some approaches attempt to predict speculative attacks, rather than only currency crises. That is, they target failed as well as successful attacks. For example, Kaminsky, Lizondo, and Reinhart (1998) combine information on reserve changes and exchange rate changes into a crisis index.[14] Models that also predict failed attacks are more useful to policymakers since they are interested in anticipating any speculative attacks, which, of course, ex ante cannot be known as failures or successes. Whether or not a devaluation occurs depends on the resolve of the authorities and the measures they take.

A difficulty with most empirical definitions of crisis arises from the need to distinguish currency crises from nominal devaluations associated with high inflation. Frankel and Rose (1996) restricted the definition of crisis to include only cases when

---

[13] Eichengreen, Rose, and Wyplosz (1995); Frankel and Rose (1996); Kaminsky and Reinhart (1999); and Milesi-Ferretti and Razin (1998) use event studies in addition to other approaches. See also Moreno (1995).

[14] Studies analyzing advanced economies, such as Eichengreen, Rose, and Wyplosz (1995), typically combine information on interest rate changes, reserve changes, and exchange rate changes into an index of speculative attack. This is generally not possible for developing countries because historical data on market interest rates are often not available.

the nominal devaluation was at least 10 percent higher than the previous year. This definition does not work very well in cases of high inflation; for example, it would consider a country to have a crisis if it had a constant annual inflation rate of 80 percent and a nominal depreciation of 74 percent one year and 85 percent the next. Kaminsky, Lizondo, and Reinhart (1998) follow an alternative approach that basically takes different benchmarks to define a crisis in periods of very high inflation (observations in which the country had a six-month inflation rate above 150 percent).

The studies this paper analyzes combine different elements: a selection of countries, a methodology for the estimation, and a definition of crisis. We try to make the selection of countries homogeneous across studies, but we maintain the "original" definition of crisis (25 percent depreciation for Frankel-Rose, and so on) so as to follow the original study as closely as possible. As mentioned above with reference to the Frankel-Rose study, focusing on a smaller set of more homogeneous developing countries does affect the results.[15] In addition, it should be highlighted that the definition of crisis is not uncontroversial: as already mentioned earlier, the Frankel-Rose definition considers high inflation/depreciation episodes as currency crises and the Kaminsky-Reinhart method defines low inflation episodes as those with six-month inflation below 150 percent, implying that only hyperinflationary episodes get classified as high inflation ones. Of course, other approaches that follow the same methodology but change the definition of crisis are also possible. For example, Milesi-Ferretti and Razin (1998) consider alternative definitions of crises within the Frankel-Rose framework, focusing in particular on depreciation episodes that follow periods of relative exchange rate stability. While the overlap between the different definitions of crises is still fairly substantial, some of the results actually change.[16] Esquivel and Larraín (1998) also use panel techniques with annual data to explore the determinants of currency crises, but they define a crisis based on higher-frequency (that is, monthly) changes in the *real* exchange rate (so as not to give undue weight to high-inflation episodes).[17]

How to Generate Predictions

Once a set of crises has been identified, the question arises what methodology to use to predict the crises. One can divide the possible frameworks into three groups. The first approach is to analyze a particular crisis episode or set of crises that occur together in time. Sachs, Tornell, and Velasco (1999a), for example, analyze the incidence of currency crisis across a group of countries after the Mexican crisis as a function of a variety of precrisis factors. This approach cannot hope to shed light on the timing of crises. Rather, it may answer the question of which countries are most likely to suffer serious attacks in the event of an unfavorable change in the global environment. The justification for this approach is twofold. First, the timing of a crisis may be much harder to predict than its incidence across a group of countries. Knowing which country is most vulnerable in the event of a worldwide shock could still be useful information. Second, by focusing on a set of crises occurring at one particular time, the model avoids the problem posed by the possible changes in the determinants of crisis episodes over time. However, although this type of model may help to identify more vulnerable countries, its specification limits its usefulness for predicting future crises.[18]

The remaining two approaches examine data on a sample of countries through time (that is, a "panel" of data). The "indicators" approach of Kaminsky, Lizondo, and Reinhart (1998) considers a number of indicator variables (such as the degree of real exchange rate overvaluation) and calculates threshold values such that the indicator issues a "signal" of forthcoming crisis when its value is above this threshold. The third method, exemplified by Frankel and Rose (1996), uses a regression in which the dependent variable takes a value of unity when there is a crisis and zero otherwise (called a probit regression). The independent variables are the various potential predictors suggested by economic theory.[19]

---

[15]See Berg and Pattillo (1999a) and Milesi-Ferretti and Razin (1998) for more details.

[16]For example, using the original Frankel-Rose definition it is found that countries with an exchange rate peg are less likely to suffer a currency crisis. This result, however, does not hold when the definition of crisis is changed. The reason is that countries with high inflation (which are "overrepresented" in the sample of currency crises using the basic Frankel-Rose definition) typically do not (cannot) peg their exchange rates.

[17]They find that an appreciated real exchange rate, high current account deficits, and a low ratio of reserves to broad money, among other indicators, increase the probability of a crisis.

[18]Glick and Rose (1998) look at crises in several cross sections of countries in years of widespread currency crises. They find that the incidence of crisis across countries is partly explained by trade linkages with the country that initiated the round of contagion (for example, Mexico in 1994–95). This would not help predict and does not even help with relative vulnerabilities, unless one knows which country initiates the contagion.

[19]A recent development is models produced by several investment banks to forecast the probabilities of large currency depreciations. The banks' studies seek to provide information that could be profitable to participants in foreign exchange markets, often using models similar to those in the third category above. (See *Event Risk Indicator Handbook* of J.P. Morgan, *Emerging Markets Risk Indicator* of Credit Suisse First Boston, *Emerging Markets Strategy* of Lehman Brothers, *Early Warning System* of Citicorp, and *GS-Watch* of Goldman Sachs.)

There are important additional design issues for methods such as the indicators and probit regression approaches that attempt to predict both the timing and the cross-country incidence of crises. First, a choice must be made regarding how far in advance the prediction is to be made. Kaminsky, Lizondo, and Reinhart (1998), for example, attempt not to predict the exact timing of the crisis but rather the likelihood that a crisis will occur some time in the next 24 months. Although this relatively wide time window could be considered a drawback of the method, it may be a realistic approach, particularly in light of the discussion in Section II that suggested that the timing of crises may not be predictable at all in conditions of multiple equilibria and self-fulfilling attacks.

A further question involves what set of historical crises to use in calibrating the model. The inclusion of more years and more countries would in principle allow more precise estimation of the relationship between the various predictive variables and subsequent crises. However, the crises used to estimate the model must be reasonably similar to the crises the model is trying to predict. Different approaches can be distinguished along this dimension. The Sachs, Tornell, and Velasco (1996a) cross-section approach represents one extreme, in which no historical information is used, with the model being fit to only one set of crises occurring in a fairly small sample of similar countries at one point in time. At the other extreme are the approaches of Kaminsky, Lizondo, and Reinhart (1998) and Frankel and Rose (1996). Both use data from as far back as 1970. Frankel and Rose, in addition, use data from as many countries as possible, over 100. Evidence suggests that this sample is too large and diverse, in that the impact of various determinants on the probability of crises in a smaller set of more homogeneous developing countries can be more reliably estimated.[20]

What Variables to Include and How to Measure Them?

The discussion of the nature of currency crises in Section II suggests a large number of variables that might help predict currency crises. Indeed, a variety of predictive variables have been considered for inclusion in early warning systems. These variables can be classified into several groups. First, measures of the exchange rate itself, typically assessing the overvaluation of the real exchange rate compared with a trend or its long-term average. Second, various measures of macroeconomic imbalances, such as fiscal deficits and output growth, in the spirit of the "first-generation" crisis models discussed above. Third, variables designed to capture unsustainable external positions, such as reserve adequacy measures, external debt, and the size of the current account deficit. Fourth, problems in the domestic financial sectors; given the difficulties in obtaining measures in a consistent way across countries and time, rather crude measures have been applied such as growth rates and levels of domestic credit as indicators of overleverage. Fifth, indicators that reflect market expectations, such as interest rate differentials or the forward exchange rate.[21] Sixth, financial market contagion variables, such as the number of crises in recent months in other countries.[22]

For the purpose of estimation of an early warning system, a given variable must be reasonably comparable across time and countries. Many factors that experience suggests might help predict crises are not easily measured and do not meet that standard. Perhaps the most glaring examples involve data regarding the health of financial systems, such as rates of nonperforming loans and capital adequacy. Similarly, variables may be badly mismeasured for various reasons. Accurate and comprehensive information on short-term external debt of the private sector, for example, is not available for most countries. These measurement or availability problems imply that it is difficult to incorporate this information into early warning systems that are calibrated using historical episodes.

---

[20]See Milesi-Ferretti and Razin (1998) and Berg and Pattillo (1999a).

[21]This approach has the disadvantage that it cannot do better than the market itself, whereas one of the goals of a warning system is to provide *early* warning. As we saw in Section II, market expectations of crisis typically do not rise until very shortly before the crisis.

[22]Another potentially important category of variables, not included in the studies considered here, are political variables, such as the timing of elections.

IV How Well Do the Models Perform?

Recent work claiming success in predicting crises has concentrated almost exclusively on in-sample prediction.[23] There is an important danger in focusing on this type of evaluation as it may overestimate the ability of the models to predict future crises. The implementation of each model involves using historical data to estimate the model, that is to decide exactly how much weight to give to each of the predictive variables. The danger is that, as emphasized in Section II, different sets of crises may be fundamentally different. Models fitted over historical data may not provide much guidance for the prediction of subsequent crises. To guard against overestimating the usefulness of these crisis-prediction models, we emphasize the testing of these models "out of sample," that is in predicting crises that occurred after the models were formulated and estimated.

The Asian crisis is a natural testing ground for the out-of-sample performance of crisis-prediction models. The high number of crises in 1997 came largely as a surprise to most observers, suggesting a possible role for prediction models. These crises contained a variety of new elements as well as some important points of continuity with previous crises. Moreover, a number of crisis-prediction models had been elaborated prior to the Asian crisis, inspired by the Mexican crisis of 1994. Thus, this section addresses the question: if one had used these models in late 1996, how well armed would one have been to predict the Asian crisis?

To evaluate the performance of early warning systems, one study representative of each of the three types of approaches to predicting currency crises that were identified above is examined in depth. These studies are among the most well known and promising based on their success within sample. All these models were formulated prior to 1997, so that their application to the Asian crisis is truly out of sample. In addition, the results from a model currently under development in the Developing Country Studies Division of the IMF's Research Department (DCSD),[24] which combines features of the other three approaches, are also presented. Out-of-sample tests of this model can be performed only in the sense of estimating it using data up to 1995 and then checking how well it fares in predicting events in 1997. This is not a "pure" out-of-sample test, however, in that the model was inevitably formulated, and, in particular, variables chosen, with the benefit of hindsight regarding the Asian crisis. The models have the following features.

- Kaminsky, Lizondo, and Reinhart (1998) (KLR) develop an early warning system for currency crises based on a variety of monthly indicators that signal a crisis whenever they cross a certain threshold value. A variable-by-variable approach is chosen so that a surveillance system based on the method would provide assessments of which variables are "out-of-line." The information from the separate variables is combined to produce a composite measure of the probability of crisis.
- Frankel and Rose's (1996) (FR) probit regression model of currency crashes analyzes a broad set of potentially important variables. Motivated by the Mexican crisis, the study tests in particular the hypothesis that certain characteristics of capital inflows are associated with currency crashes. Their use of annual data permits them to look at these variables, as well as others that are available only at annual frequency.
- Sachs, Tornell, and Velasco (1996a) (STV) restrict their attention to a cross-section of countries in 1995. They test whether the incidence and severity of crisis following the devaluation of the Mexican peso can be explained by a particular set of fundamentals, where the framework assumes that countries with weak fundamentals and low reserves were particularly vulnerable to the effects of Mexico's devaluation.[25]

---

[23]Partial exceptions are Tornell (1998) and Kaminsky (1998).

[24]The findings in this chapter are based on Berg and Pattillo (1999a).

[25]Their approach has also been applied to the Asian crisis. Tornell (1998), Radelet and Sachs (1998b), and Corsetti and others (1998) estimate variants of STV for 1997. IMF (1998) constructs a composite indicator of crisis based on the STV approach and argues that it accords well with the pattern of country experience in the Asian crisis.

- The DCSD model, in the spirit of the KLR approach, uses monthly data to determine which variables contribute to the probability of a crisis occurring within the following 24 months. The concept is to take maximum advantage of the predictive power provided by the monthly indicators suggested by KLR, as well as some additional variables, by using them in an econometric framework similar to that of FR (a probit regression).

The most basic evaluation of the models is to gauge how well they perform in predicting crises in-sample, that is, when applied to the historical data that was used to formulate the model. The discussion below is based on estimation of the KLR, STV, and DCSD models on a common sample of 23 emerging market economies through April 1995 and on a sample of 41 developing countries for FR.[26]

Kaminsky-Lizondo-Reinhart Model

Since the KLR approach assesses the signaling properties of indicators one at a time, the effectiveness of the approach can be examined by determining the extent to which each individual indicator is useful in predicting crises. Of the 15 indicators considered (see Table 2), 8 are found to be informative, in that crises are more likely to occur when the indicator signals than when it does not. These "good" indicators are deviations of the real exchange rate from trend, the growth in the ratio of M2 to international reserves, export growth, growth of international reserves, "excess" M1 balances, growth in domestic credit as a fraction of GDP, the real interest rate, and the change in terms of trade.

Table 2 shows various measures of the effectiveness of these indicators. First, consider the observations that are in fact followed by a crisis within 24 months. Column (1) shows the fraction of these observations for which the indicator is signaling a crisis. Next consider false alarms, that is signals that are not followed by a crisis within 24 months. Column (2) shows the fraction of signals that are false alarms. A perfect indicator would obtain 100 percent in column (1), implying that a signal was issued every month during the 24 months prior to each crisis, and 0 in column (2), indicating that all signals that were issued were indeed followed by a crisis within 24 months. Clearly, some indicators are better than others. The best eight would seem to contain useful information; for these indicators, the issuance of a signal implies a probability of crisis higher than

that implied by the actual incidence of crises over the sample, as shown in column (4). On average, these good indicators signal a crisis 18 percent of the time a crisis does in fact ensue.[27] A large share of the signals are bad signals: 71 percent of the times that the average good indicator signaled, it was not followed by a crisis within 24 months.

These results appear to be poor: signals are mostly false alarms, while most precrisis months are not signaled. However, these signals do carry substantial information about the probability of crisis. When an indicator signals, a crisis ensues more often than when there is no signal. For example, 47 percent of the time the real exchange rate signals, a crisis ensues within 24 months, as column (3) of Table 2 shows. This probability of crisis is much higher than the average frequency of crises in the sample, so that the real exchange rate signal does increase the expected probability of crisis, as shown in column (4).

Clearly, it would be desirable to combine the information from the various indicators. To this end, the indicators can be aggregated into a composite index that measures the probability of crisis for each country at every point in time (see Kaminsky, 1998). Table 2 showed that some indicators are much better predictors than others. Thus, each indicator is weighted by a measure of its reliability in predicting crises. The performance of this approach can be assessed systematically by looking at various goodness-of-fit measures (Box 1 explains these measures in detail). For example, a natural question to pose is whether the estimated probability of crisis is above 50 percent prior to actual crises. Table 3 shows that the predicted probability of crisis was above 50 percent in 9 percent of the months between January 1970 to April 1995 when a crisis followed within 24 months. The model does correctly call almost all (99 percent) of the more numerous tranquil periods. One could consider a lower cutoff probability than 50 percent if there is relatively higher concern with missing crises and relatively lower concern with issuing false alarms. Using a 25 percent cutoff, for example, the model predicts a crisis in 46 percent of periods that it should.[28] Of course, this improvement in the fraction of crises correctly predicted comes at the expense of a lower fraction of tranquil periods correctly called.

Another way of looking at these goodness-of-fit statistics comes from taking the perspective of a de-

---

[26]The countries in the different samples are listed in footnotes to Table 3.

[27]An alternative, less exacting benchmark would be to consider a crisis as correctly called whenever an indicator signaled "at least once" within the 24 months prior to each crisis. On this measure, the average good indicator signaled before 66 percent of the crises.

[28]More precisely, the model issued a signal in 46 percent of the months in the two years prior to each crisis.

Table 2. Performance of Kaminsky-Lizondo-Reinhart (KLR) Indicators

	Good Signals as a Share of Times the Indicator Should Be Signaling[1] (1)	False Alarms as a Share of Signals[2] (2)	Probability of Crisis Given a Signal (3)	Increase in Expected Probability if Indicator Signals (In percentage points)[3] (4)
Real exchange rate[4]	26	53	47	29
M2/reserves growth rate	26	65	35	17
International reserves growth rate	18	67	33	15
Export growth rate	15	73	27	9
Excess M1 balances	15	73	27	9
Real interest rate	15	78	22	4
Domestic credit/GDP growth rate	19	78	22	4
Terms of trade growth rate	10	80	20	1
Lending rate/deposit rate	9	85	15	−1
M2 multiplier growth rate	17	85	15	−2
Industrial production growth rate	13	82	18	−2
Import growth rate	12	84	16	−2
Real interest differential	14	86	14	−4
Stock price index growth rate	13	87	13	−6
Bank deposit growth rate	7	88	12	−6
Average for 8 "good" indicators[5]	18	71	29	11

Sources: Berg and Pattillo (1999a), and IMF staff calculations.
[1]A good signal is a signal that is followed by a crisis within 24 months.
[2]A false alarm is a signal that is not followed by a crisis within 24 months.
[3]Probability of crisis given a signal less the unconditional probability of crisis in the sample.
[4]Deviation from trend.
[5]"Good" indicators are those for which signals are in fact associated with a higher frequency of crisis. That is, for good indicators, a signal implies a probability of crisis higher than that implied by the actual incidence of crisis over the sample.

cision maker who must choose a course of action based on these crisis predictions. An important question would be the incidence of false alarms—the fraction of times no crisis occurs when crises are predicted. When probabilities above 25 percent are said to be predicting a crisis, 65 percent of these crisis predictions precede noncrisis months. As we observed before, this high false alarm rate does not mean the estimated probabilities carry no information. Most of the time, the estimated probability of crisis is below 25 percent. Crises in fact follow these observations only 13 percent of the time. When the probability rises above 25 percent, crises are in fact more likely, ensuing 35 percent of the time.

Frankel-Rose Model

The FR model was updated through 1996 using a sample of 41 countries that is comparable to the samples used in the other studies (the original study was based in a much broader sample of developing countries). The results show that the probability of a crisis increases when domestic credit growth is high, reserves as a share of broad money are low, the real exchange rate is overvalued, the fiscal and current account deficits are high, the economy is more closed (measured by the share of exports and imports in GDP), and foreign interest rates are high. In addition, some characteristics of capital inflows

---

Box 1.   Summary Measures of Model Performance

One of the difficulties in assessing the predictive success of early warning systems is that the models generally produce an estimated probability of crisis that cannot be compared with the unobservable actual probability of crisis but only with the occurrence or not of a crisis. Yet it is possible to compute a number of measures of how well model probabilities correspond to the subsequent incidence of crises (goodness-of-fit). The first step is to convert predicted probabilities of crisis into alarms or signals that a crisis will ensue within the following 24 months (assuming that 24 months is the model's horizon). A signal is defined as a predicted probability of crisis above some threshold level (the cutoff threshold). Then, each observation (a particular country in a particular month—for example, Thailand in December 1996) is categorized as to whether it is predicted to be a precrisis month and also according to whether it is an actual precrisis month.

It is a predicted precrisis observation if the predicted probability of crisis is above the threshold; otherwise it is a predicted tranquil observation. If a crisis in fact ensues within 24 months of the observation in question, it is an actual precrisis observation; otherwise it is an actual tranquil observation.

The accompanying table shows how the signals from the DCSD model discussed in Section IV and presented in Table 5 compare to actual outcomes, for the out-of-sample period May 1995 through December 1997. It uses a cutoff threshold for calling a crisis of 25 percent.

Each number represents the number of observations that satisfy the criteria listed in the rows and columns. Thus, a given observation is either followed by a crisis within 24 months or it is not, so it belongs in either the tranquil column or the precrisis column. The model either generates a probability of crisis below 25 percent or it does not, so it is counted in either the tranquil row or the precrisis row. For example, for the entire out-of-sample period and country sample, there were a total of 321 tranquil months, and for 259 of them the probabil-

ity of crisis was below the 25 percent threshold. From this table the various measures of accuracy discussed in the text can be calculated:

Out-of-Sample Goodness-of-Fit: DCSD Model

Predicted	Actual		
	Tranquil	Precrisis	Total
Tranquil	259	32	291
Precrisis	62	88	150
Total	321	120	441

- The fraction of observations correctly called (79 percent) is equal to the sum of precrisis months correctly called (observations that were followed by a crisis within 24 months for which a signal was issued) (88) and tranquil periods correctly called (259) divided by the total number of observations (441).

- The rate of false alarms as a share of signals (41 percent) is equal to the number of predicted crises not in fact followed by a crisis (62) divided by the total number of observations for which the model predicted a crisis (150).

- The probability of a crisis given a signal (59 percent) is equal to the number of observations for which a signal was issued and a crisis ensued (88) divided by the total number of signals issued (150). (This is the same as 100 minus the rate of false alarms.)

- The probability of a crisis given no signal (11 percent) is equal to the number of observations for which a signal was not issued and a crisis ensued (32) divided by the total number of observations during which no signal was issued (291). The difference between the probability of crisis given a signal and the probability of crisis given no signal is the increase in the risk of crisis associated with the issuance of a signal.

---

seem to matter. Low shares of concessional debt and foreign direct investment as a proportion of total debt increase the probability of crisis, as do high shares of debt issued by the public sector.

The goodness-of-fit statistics show that the model performs fairly well in generating predicted probabilities of crashes above 50 percent when a crash actually occurs (column 2 of Table 3). The model correctly predicts one-third of the crashes in the sample, with only a 26 percent incidence of false alarms. Using a threshold of 25 percent, correct predictions increase to 63 percent of the crashes and false alarms to 52 percent. Thus, the FR model performs somewhat better than the KLR framework in predicting crises within sample.

Sachs-Tornell-Velasco Model

STV argue that a key feature of the 1995 crises was that the attacks only hit hard at already vulnerable countries. Thus, countries with overvalued exchange rates and weak banking systems[29] were subject to more severe attacks, but only if they had low reserves relative to monetary liabilities (so that they could not easily accommodate capital outflows) and

---

[29]Weak banking systems are proxied in a somewhat crude way by the presence of a "lending boom" under the view that rapid expansion of bank assets is associated with a deterioration of the quality of those assets.

Table 3. Predictive Power of Kaminsky-Lizondo-Reinhart (KLR), Frankel-Rose (FR), and Developing Country Studies Division (DCSD) Models—In-Sample[1]

	Full Sample			1986–April 1995 Sample
	KLR weighted-sum-based probabilities	FR probabilities	DCSD probabilities without short-term debt	DCSD probabilities with short-term debt
Goodness-of-fit (cutoff probability of 50 percent)				
Percent of observations correctly called	83	90	84	85
Percent of precrisis periods correctly called[2]	9	33	7	2
Percent of tranquil periods correctly called[3]	99	98	100	100
False alarms as percent of total alarms[4]	30	26	11	0
Probability of crisis given				
An alarm[5]	70	74	89	100
No alarm[6]	17	10	16	15
Goodness-of-fit (cutoff probability of 25 percent)				
Percent of observations correctly called	75	86	78	81
Percent of precrisis periods correctly called[2]	46	63	48	39
Percent of tranquil periods correctly called[3]	81	89	84	88
False alarms as percent of total alarms[4]	65	52	63	64
Probability of crisis given				
An alarm[5]	35	48	37	36
No alarm[6]	13	6	11	11

Sources: Berg and Pattillo (1999a), and IMF staff calculations.

[1]The KLR and DCSD models are estimated using a 23-country or economy sample consisting of Argentina, Bolivia, Brazil, Chile, Colombia, India, Indonesia, Israel, Jordan, Korea, Malaysia, Mexico, Pakistan, Peru, the Philippines, South Africa, Sri Lanka, Taiwan Province of China, Thailand, Turkey, Uruguay, Venezuela, and Zimbabwe.

The 41-country FR sample includes all of the above except for Israel, Jordan, South Africa, and Taiwan Province of China, plus the following 22 countries: Algeria, Botswana, Costa Rica, Côte d'Ivoire, the Dominican Republic, Ecuador, Egypt, El Salvador, Guatemala, Hungary, the Islamic Republic of Iran, Jamaica, Mauritius, Morocco, Oman, Panama, Portugal, Paraguay, Romania, the Syrian Arab Republic, Trinidad and Tobago, and Tunisia.

[2]This is the number of precrisis periods correctly called (observations for which the estimated probability of crisis is above the cutoff probability and a crisis ensues within 24 months) as a share of total precrisis periods.

[3]This is the number of tranquil periods correctly called (observations for which the estimated probability of crisis is below the cutoff probability and no crisis ensues within 24 months) as a share of total tranquil periods.

[4]A false alarm is an observation with an estimated probability of crisis above the cut off (an alarm) not followed by a crisis within 24 months.

[5]This is the number of precrisis periods correctly called as a share of total predicted precrisis periods (observations for which the estimated probability of crisis is above the cutoff probability).

[6]This is the number of periods where tranquility is predicted and a crisis actually ensues as a share of total predicted tranquil periods (observations for which the estimated probability of crisis is below the cutoff probability).

weak fundamentals (so that fighting the attack with higher interest rates would be too costly).

Using the 23-country common sample (still for the 1995 crises), the estimated STV model fits the data only moderately well. The main hypotheses receive mixed support: a depreciated real exchange rate lowers the severity of a crisis only for countries

with low reserves and weak fundamentals, but the effect of lending booms on such countries is insignificant.[30]

_____

[30]The original STV results, with a slightly different sample, are more successful in fitting the 1994–95 crises.

Since the model does not predict the discrete event of whether a country has a crisis or not, but rather the level of an index of exchange market and reserve pressure, it is not possible to assess how well the model fits the data in terms of a proportion of crises correctly called, as done for the other studies. The STV framework predicts which countries should face the greatest pressure on the crisis index during a period of global financial turbulence such as the Mexican crisis.[31] This suggests evaluating the performance of the model by comparing rankings of countries based on the predicted and actual crisis indices, as shown in Table 4. One would expect the predicted rankings to match up relatively well with the actual rankings, since these are in-sample predictions, that is, predictions for the period that the model was designed to explain. Indeed, the table shows that there is a positive and significant correlation between the actual and predicted crisis indices. However, less than one-quarter of the variation in actual rankings is explained by the predicted rankings.

Developing Country Studies Division Model

The DCSD model uses monthly data to determine which variables contribute to the probability of a crisis occurring within the following 24 months. The probability of this event is estimated in a probit regression model. This has two advantages: the model can aggregate predictive variables more satisfactorily into a composite probability, taking account of correlations among different variables; and it is easy to test for the statistical significance of individual variables. In addition, it is possible to allow the risk of a crisis to increase linearly with the predictor variables.[32]

The model is obtained by including the 15 KLR variables (where sufficient data were available) plus three additional variables, then simplifying by dropping insignificant variables.[33] The additional variables are the level of M2/reserves, the current account to GDP ratio, and the ratio of short-term

debt to reserves. The results indicate that the more significant variables are the real exchange rate relative to trend, the current account deficit, reserve growth, export growth, and the ratio of short-term debt to reserves.

The DCSD model excluding short-term debt performs about as well in-sample as the KLR model, as shown in Table 3. Because the variable is only available from 1986, the model that includes this variable is estimated over a shorter period. The in-sample performance is somewhat worse in this specification than for the model excluding short-term debt. Using a 25 percent cutoff, the model including short-term debt to reserves predicts a crisis 39 percent of the times that it should, while 64 percent of alarms are false.

Out-of-Sample Performance: 1997

For an early warning system to be a useful tool, it would have to provide informative signals out of sample, namely, beyond the time period for which the model itself was estimated. An interesting (although by no means complete) test of the out-of-sample performance of the models reviewed here is to check whether they produced signals of impending trouble ahead of the crises of 1997 using only the data available before the crisis. Because the maximum prediction horizon of KLR and DCSD is two years, these models were estimated using only data through April 1995 to forecast crisis probabilities for 1997 and to compare those forecasts with the outcomes. FR was estimated using annual data through 1996, and STV through April 1995.

The out-of-sample performance of the models can be evaluated in two ways. First, a natural assessment of the model performance is to check whether the models predicted high probabilities of crisis (above say, 50 or 25 percent) in the periods preceding actual crises. This goodness-of-fit test evaluates the success in predicting the *timing* of crises. Second, given the rather unpredictable nature of the timing of global turbulence and contagion, the models can be put to the test of predicting the relative severity of crises (or, more precisely, measures of balance of payments pressure) faced by different developing countries. That is, one would judge the success of the models by how they anticipated—again using only previously available information—the relative intensity of balance of payments pressures suffered by different countries. The performance of the models is then assessed by comparing a ranking of countries according to the value of their crisis index as predicted by the models with their ranking using actual data for 1997.

The first type of test, evaluating whether the models predicted probabilities of crisis accurately, was

---

[31]The objective of the original STV exercise was largely to explain, not predict, the incidence of crises. Tornell (1998) and others have used the same framework with a more explicit predictive intent.

[32]The KLR approach, in contrast, assumes that the probability of crisis in the subsequent 24 months is a step function of the value of the indicator, equal to 0 when the indicator variable is below the threshold and equal to 1 at or above the threshold. Berg and Pattillo (1999b) found that a probit model with variables entered linearly had somewhat higher predictive power than the pure threshold framework.

[33]See Berg and Pattillo (1999b) for a full discussion of the specification and estimation of the DCSD model.

Table 4. Correlation of Actual and Predicted Rankings Based on Sachs-Tornell-Velasco (STV) Approach: In-Sample

	Actual[1]		Predicted	
	Crisis severity	Rank	Crisis severity	Rank
Mexico	791.32	1	293.57	2
Argentina	202.09	2	322.11	1
Brazil	197.01	3	186.05	4
Uruguay	85.03	4	74.57	7
Philippines	71.87	5	168.08	5
Venezuela	51.65	6	12.89	10
Taiwan Province of China	44.00	7	69.61	8
Colombia	42.29	8	49.25	9
South Africa	22.32	9	−1.50	11
Zimbabwe	15.79	10	−85.30	23
Indonesia	13.15	11	−19.23	17
Sri Lanka	7.37	12	−27.88	19
Pakistan	6.77	13	−35.80	20
India	−12.28	14	−11.48	15
Jordan	−15.64	15	−36.76	21
Thailand	−18.19	16	78.59	6
Turkey	−24.92	17	−16.96	16
Malaysia	−26.24	18	−5.88	13
Peru	−26.86	19	−36.86	22
Korea	−37.01	20	−26.00	18
Chile	−56.17	21	−3.68	12
Bolivia	−63.77	22	241.11	3
Israel	−91.40	23	−10.37	14
Correlation[2]				0.49
p-value				0.018
R^2				0.24

Source: IMF staff calculations.

[1]Actual crisis (November 1994–April 1995).

[2]Spearman Rank correlation of the fitted values and the actual crisis index and its p-value. The R^2 is from a regression of fitted values on actual values.

applied to the KLR and DCSD models only because it was not possible to produce meaningful goodness-of-fit measures of this kind for the FR and STV models, for different reasons. According to the FR definition, there are no actual crises in 1997, so there are no crises to predict. This odd result illustrates the fact that the use of annual data does not work well for the crisis variable in 1997. Because the largest depreciations happened toward the end of the year, none of the Asian countries is identified as a crisis country in 1997 within this framework.[34] The problem with the STV framework is that it does not predict the timing of discrete crisis events, but rather predicts which countries should face the greatest pressure as mea-

sured by a crisis index during a period of global financial turbulence. Thus, this model cannot be subjected to the first test because it is not possible to extract from it a prediction of the probability of crisis, although it is ideally designed for ranking countries by their level of risk, as in the second test.

The out-of-sample performance of the KLR model is less successful than the in-sample performance though also more selective as Table 5 shows. With a 25 percent probability cutoff, the KLR-based predicted probabilities correctly signal 34 percent of the crisis observations (as opposed to almost one-half within sample), while the incidence of false alarms falls to 51 percent.[35] From the perspective of

---

[34]Actually, a few countries came very close to meeting the FR conditions for identification of a crisis, most notably Indonesia and Turkey.

[35]It is remarkable that, applying a probability cutoff of 50 percent, the predictions generated on the basis of the KLR model do not forecast *any* crisis in the whole May 1995–December 1997 period.

Table 5. Predictive Power of Kaminsky-Lizondo-Reinhart and Developing Country Studies Division Models: Out-of-Sample

	KLR Weighted-Sum-Based Probabilities	DCSD Probabilities
Goodness-of-fit (cutoff probability of 50 percent)		
Percent of observations correctly called	70	74
Percent of precrisis periods correctly called[1]	0	3
Percent of tranquil periods correctly called[2]	100	100
False alarms as percent of total alarms [3]	No crisis predictions	0
Probability of crisis given		
An alarm[4]	0	100
No alarm[5]	29	27
Goodness-of-fit (cutoff probability of 25 percent)		
Percent of observations correctly called	70	79
Percent of precrisis periods correctly called[1]	34	73
Percent of tranquil periods correctly called[2]	86	81
False alarms as percent of total alarms[3]	51	41
Probability of crisis given		
An alarm[4]	49	59
No alarm[5]	24	11

Sources: Berg and Pattillo (1999a), and IMF staff calculations.

[1]This is the number of precrisis periods correctly called (observations for which the estimated probability of crisis is above the cutoff probability and a crisis ensues within 24 months) as a share of total precrisis periods.

[2]This is the number of tranquil periods correctly called (observations for which the estimated probability of crisis is below the cutoff probability and no crisis ensues within 24 months) as a share of total tranquil periods.

[3]A false alarm is an observation with an estimated probability of crisis above the cutoff (an alarm) not followed by a crisis within 24 months.

[4]This is the number of precrisis periods correctly called as a share of total predicted precrisis periods (observations for which the estimated probability of crisis is above the cutoff probability).

[5]This is the number of periods where tranquility is predicted and a crisis actually ensues as a share of total predicted tranquil periods (observations for which the estimated probability of crisis is below the cutoff probability).

a decision maker attempting to interpret the signals coming from the model, the model continues to provide predictions of some value, even out of sample. For observations in which the predicted probability of approaching crisis was below 25 percent, crises actually followed 24 percent of the time. When the predicted probability of crisis was above 25 percent, however, crises ensued 49 percent of the time.

The DCSD model performs much better out-of-sample. Again, with the 25 percent cutoff probability it correctly predicts a crisis in 73 percent of the observations that are actually followed by crises. Less

than half the time that a crisis was predicted, no crisis ensued within 24 months. The contribution of the model to the analysis of the external risk faced by the countries can be appreciated in the following way. The predicted probability of crisis was below 25 percent during most of the out-of-sample period under consideration. For these observations, crises actually occurred only 11 percent of the time. When the predicted probability of crisis was above 25 percent, however, crises ensued 59 percent of the time.

This good performance is illustrated by examining all the countries that experienced a crisis in 1997.

Except for Philippines, the probabilities were above 25 percent for most of the 24 months preceding the first month of the crisis. Looking at countries that did not experience a crisis shows that false alarms were a bigger problem for some countries than others. For Argentina, the probabilities were above 25 percent in only one of the 20 months from May 1995 to December 1996, but in 11 for Peru.

The second test focuses on the success of the models in identifying which countries would be vulnerable in a period of global financial turmoil such as 1997. The question here is whether the models assign higher predicted probabilities of crisis to those countries that had the biggest crises (as defined by each model).[36] This can be addressed by comparing how closely the predicted ranking resembles the actual one, as shown in Table 6. An additional benefit of the ranking comparison is that it provides a unified method to evaluate the forecasting performance of all four models. Clearly, a model forecasts successfully if countries that have the highest predicted probabilities of crisis are those that also display the highest values in the severity of crisis index. Thus, the table displays the correlation between the actual and predicted rankings, as well as the proportion of the variance in the actual rankings that is explained by the predicted rankings.

The rankings generated from predictions based on the four models are all positively correlated with the actual rankings according to developments in 1997. Yet the correlation is not very high, as it varies from 12 percent to 53 percent. The two models based on monthly indicators (KLR and DCSD) seem to do somewhat better according to this test, as they show higher correlation and statistical significance. Some of the models attach fairly high risk to the Asian economies and Brazil, which also experienced large reserve losses in 1997. It should be noted that the "actual" crisis rankings are based on the definition of crisis applied by each model and thus are not mutually consistent.

Summary of Effectiveness

This section has examined how well four empirical models work in predicting currency crises. The results indicate that, when an estimated probability of 25 percent or higher is taken as a prediction of a crisis, the best pure out-of-sample model correctly

predicts roughly one-half of the crises in sample, and one-third out of sample. False alarms are always common: over half the times all these models predict a crisis is approaching, no crisis occurs. Despite the high incidence of false alarms, a prediction of crisis by the model does reflect a situation of increased risk. Periods in which the model calls a crisis are substantially more likely to be followed by a crisis than periods in which the model does not call a crisis, both in sample and—to a lesser extent—out of sample.

The DCSD model performs substantially better out of sample. When this model indicates a probability of crisis above 25 percent, a crisis is in fact looming most (59 percent) of the time. And when the predicted probability of crisis is below 25 percent, a crisis in fact ensues only 11 percent of the time. Figure 3 displays the out-of-sample probabilities of crisis based on the DCSD model for a selected group of eight countries, five Asian countries and three Latin American countries. The figure shows a relatively high probability of crisis during the period preceding crises for Korea, Indonesia, Malaysia, and Thailand. The risk of crisis in the Philippines is somewhat lower but still close to the cutoff threshold. Of the Latin American countries, none of which suffered crises in 1998, only Brazil experiences a relatively high probability of crisis during this period.

It is perhaps not surprising that the DCSD model, which was formulated after the 1997 crises, performs better than the others out of sample. First, some knowledge about the 1997 crises was used to formulate the model. In particular, the inclusion of short-term external debt as a predictive variable was in part inspired by events in 1997. However, this factor should not be exaggerated. Most important, out-of-sample performance was not used as a factor in specifying the model. Another reason for the superior performance of the DCSD model is simply that as a latecomer it has benefited from a number of methodological innovations inspired by the previous models and other research, as described in Berg and Pattillo (1999b). Ultimately, only time will tell whether newer models continue to perform well in predicting future crises.

While timing seems quite difficult to predict, some of the models do better in predicting the relative severity of crisis for different countries in 1997. This suggests the models may be more useful in identifying which countries are more vulnerable in a period of international financial turmoil than in predicting the timing of currency crises. This would still be a valuable contribution of an early warning system because it could help focus attention on the countries that need policy adjustments before a crisis develops. Furthermore, comparing the relative risk faced by different countries, which may be very

---

[36]In the KLR, STV, and DCSD models, a crisis is defined to occur when a weighted average of the exchange rate depreciation and loss of reserves exceeds its average by a certain magnitude. FR define a crisis as an exchange rate depreciation of at least 25 percent that also exceeds the previous year's depreciation by at least 10 percent.

Table 6. Correlation of Actual and Predicted Rankings for 1997

	KLR		DCSD	FR		STV	
	Actual crisis index	Predicted probabilities of crisis[1]	Predicted probabilities of crisis[1]	Actual crisis index	Predicted probabilities of crisis	Actual crisis index	Predicted probabilities of crisis
Korea	1	4	9	—	—	3	11
Thailand	2	7	3	3	11	2	5
Indonesia	3	11	6	2	7	1	9
Malaysia	4	13	4	—	—	4	6
Zimbabwe	5	9	—	—	—	5	12
Philippines	6	1	17	7	8	6	1
Taiwan Province of China	7	3	1	—	—	9	22
Colombia	8	12	2	8	6	8	4
India	9	21	11	14	—	13	19
Brazil	10	2	15	10	5	14	2
Turkey	11	10	12	1	2	7	21
Venezuela	12	16	20	5	12	21	13
Pakistan	13	5	5	6	9	10	20
South Africa	14	8	7	—	—	12	16
Jordan	15	17	14	—	—	17	15
Sri Lanka	16	19	13	11	13	15	17
Chile	17	20	18	15	10	16	14
Bolivia	18	21	22	13	—	22	10
Argentina	19	18	19	16	3	23	7
Mexico	20	14	21	12	—	18	18
Peru	21	6	8	9	4	20	23
Uruguay	22	21	16	4	1	11	3
Israel	23	15	10	—	—	19	8
Correlation[2]		0.52	0.53		0.12		0.23
p-value		0.011	0.011		0.694		0.295
R^2		0.28	0.29		0.02		0.05

Sources: Berg and Pattillo (1999a), and IMF staff calculations.

[1] Average of 1996 estimates of probabilities of crisis in 1997.

[2] Spearman Rank correlation of the fitted values and the actual crisis index and its p-value. The R^2 is from a regression of fitted values on actual values.

Figure 3. 24-Month-Ahead Crisis Probabilities for Selected Countries[1]

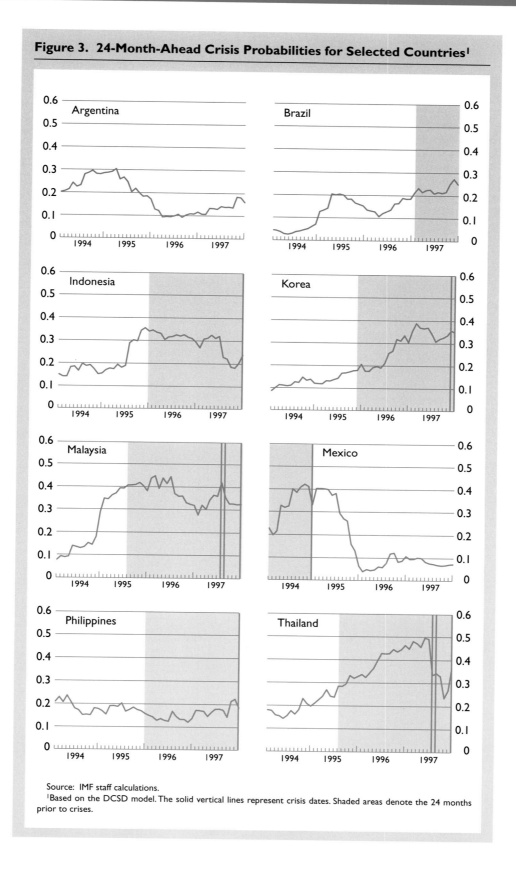

Source: IMF staff calculations.

[1]Based on the DCSD model. The solid vertical lines represent crisis dates. Shaded areas denote the 24 months prior to crises.

diverse in geographical and economic terms, is not easy to do without applying systematic quantitative techniques.

Independently of the value of the models as precise predictors of crises, the analysis of their findings provides some insight into which variables are the most important determinants of crises. All approaches demonstrate that the probability of a currency crisis increases when the real exchange rate is overvalued relative to trend, and domestic credit growth and the ratio of M2 to reserves are high. Large current account deficits and reserve losses increase the probability of crisis in all three of the methods that include these variables. High short-term debt to reserves ratios are also found to lead to an increased probability of crisis in the specifications that use this variable. Some evidence is also found for the importance of other variables, such as export growth, the size of the government budget deficit, and the share of foreign direct investment in external debt. Surprisingly, output growth was not found to be a significant predictor of crises when tested. The evidence on interest rates was mixed. High domestic real interest rates provide informative signals of impending crises while the differential between foreign and domestic real interest rates does not; yet in one specification high foreign interest rates do increase the probability of a currency crash.

V   The Implementation of an Early Warning System

While there has been a recent flurry of research on the prediction of currency crises, it is clear that more work needs to be done to better understand their causes and more successfully predict them. The empirical literature on early warning systems is relatively young, at least for models with an explicit forecasting objective, especially when compared with, say, leading indicators of business cycles or large-scale macroeconomic models that have been in development for several decades. Many ideas have not yet been explored satisfactorily, including basic issues such as the empirical definition of a crisis. It may also be possible to incorporate new variables that seem to be relevant but have not previously been available in the desired format or frequency, such as measures of nonperforming loans in the banking sector, more refined measures of short-term liabilities (including valuations of the forward and contingent positions of the monetary authorities, for example), and even the budget deficit. An important feature of currency crises that deserves further study is contagion, which is difficult to incorporate in a satisfactory way but which undoubtably plays a role at least in the timing of crises. Other issues that should be studied include institutional factors such as the strength of regulatory frameworks, corporate governance, the degree of openness of the capital account, and variables accounting for political developments. Finally, various aspects of the specification of models could be further studied to improve their reliability, including by reconsidering the most appropriate forecast horizon.

The work done to date and reviewed in Section IV nonetheless suggests that the implementation of a quantitative early warning system might be a fruitful endeavor. Early warning systems contain significant useful information and can produce estimates of the probability of crisis and rankings of the susceptibility to crisis of different countries. In particular, Section IV demonstrated that some of the models can forecast with at least a modest degree of success the timing of crises, and that they do better still at predicting the cross-country vulnerability to crisis. That is, they may help predict which country is more likely to suffer a crisis during a given period, even if they do less well at predicting how many crises there will be in that period.

A central fact relating to the use of early warning systems is that their accuracy is of necessity highly imperfect. Sections II and IV showed that while early warning systems help identify patterns common to many crises, they cannot be expected to predict with complete, or even high, accuracy. While further research can be expected to improve performance, many of the reasons for inaccuracy, detailed above, will remain. In particular, the timing of crises may be impossible to forecast as it may depend on changes in market sentiment and other inherently unpredictable events. Moreover, even a system that is highly successful from a statistical point of view would only address part of the relevant information regarding the prospects for a crisis. The analysis of the vulnerability of an economy involves many more aspects than can be summarized in a handful of generally available variables.

It should also be recognized that such an early warning system framework presumes that differences in economic structure, institutions, and so on across countries are not so important as to negate the effectiveness of a cross-country approach. However, key determinants of the likelihood of crisis may not be the same across countries, or their relative impact may differ. And the relevant factors may change over time as the level of economic development and market structures change. This suggests the use of a fairly homogeneous group of countries and sample period in the design of an early warning system to minimize such problems. For instance, these models are likely to apply better to the group of "emerging" economies that have been more active in international capital markets over the past few years.

To conclude, early warning systems should be used but not abused. This means that the primary use of such a system should be as only one tool among many others for analysis of external risks. Thus, any utilization of early warning systems must be embedded in broader analysis that takes into account all the important complexities, some of which a cross-country statistical model inevitably must ignore.

Appendix   A Survey of the Literature on Currency Crises

This appendix provides a selective review of the economic literature on currency crises, focusing on the explanations that have been advanced of the determinants and the processes leading to crises.[37]

First-Generation Models

In his seminal paper on balance of payments crises, Krugman (1979) considers a small open economy with a pegged exchange rate where domestic credit expands continuously, typically to finance a budget deficit. The peg is sustained by a positive stock of foreign exchange reserves, but reserves are gradually depleted as agents continuously buy foreign currency as a result of the imbalance between the expanding domestic credit and the stable money demand. Krugman shows that reserves will eventually be wiped out by a speculative attack once they have reached a sufficiently low level, even though there is no change in policies to trigger the attack. With well-informed, rational speculators assessing the situation, the currency attack will take place only when the transition from the pegged exchange rate to its successor system (presumed to be a float) yields the required return to speculators. Although the policy inconsistency that condemns the exchange rate system is well recognized in advance, and the eventual demise of the peg is known to be unavoidable, it is not profitable to launch an attack too early (or to wait too long). In fact, the determination of the timing of the attack is the main analytical question that first-generation models attempt to answer.

Although Krugman's model is very stylized, and may seem artificial, other models have extended his framework to capture the features usually present in balance of payments crises. With some degree of price sluggishness or the introduction of nontraded goods, the buildup to a crisis features an appreciat-

ing real exchange rate and widening current account deficits (Calvo, 1987). Introducing some degree of uncertainty, the timing of the devaluation cannot be exactly predicted and a "peso problem" emerges, that is, a persistent divergence between nominal domestic and foreign interest rates owing to the expectation of an impending devaluation (Krasker, 1980; Penati and Pennacchi, 1989).

Several empirical studies of devaluations have found common features that are consistent with the framework of first-generation models. Indeed, large devaluations in developing countries have often been preceded by expansionary fiscal and monetary policies, interest rate premia, real exchange rate appreciations, and widening current account imbalances (Edwards, 1989). Analyses of individual country experiences have also found a link between excessive credit growth and subsequent crises in a number of case studies of devaluations including in Mexico, Argentina, Italy, and France.[38]

Second-Generation Models

The breakdown of the exchange rate mechanism (ERM) of the European Monetary System (EMS) in 1993 and the Mexican crisis of 1994 spurred a reconsideration of the explanations of exchange rate crises offered by the economic literature. Some aspects of those crises were hard to reconcile with traditional models of speculative attacks for two reasons. First, as underscored by Obstfeld and Rogoff (1995) among others, the decision to abandon an exchange rate peg in the context of the ERM crises was not due to the exhaustion of foreign exchange reserves, but to the reluctance of governments to fight prolonged speculative attacks with high interest rates. In this regard, the second-generation models explain speculative attacks in a context in which the

---

[37]For comprehensive reviews of the theoretical and empirical literature, see Garber and Svensson (1995) and Flood and Marion (1998a). Agénor, Bhandari, and Flood (1992) provide a useful survey of the literature on first-generation speculative attacks.

[38]See Blanco and Garber (1986) and Goldberg (1994) for Mexico, Connolly (1986) and Cumby and van Wijnbergen (1989) for Argentina, and Penati and Pennacchi (1989) for Italy and France.

government decisions take into account the costs and benefits involved in abandoning the peg. In contrast, first-generation models provide no explicit rationale for government policy actions.

The second reason for reassessing theories of currency crises was the unexpected and apparently inexplicable nature of some of these crises, which led several observers to suggest the possibility that self-fulfilling expectations may have played a prominent role (see Eichengreen and Wyplosz (1993) for an interpretation of the EMS crisis along those lines, and Sachs, Tornell, and Velasco (1996b) and Cole and Kehoe (1996) for such an interpretation of the Mexican crisis). For example, France was subject to repeated speculative attacks that led to a widening of the fluctuation band vis-à-vis the deutsche mark, even though traditional "fundamentals" were not visibly out of line—France had modest fiscal imbalances, its real exchange rate had not appreciated, and it was running a current account surplus.

But how can self-fulfilling crises occur? The key feature is the link between the government's assessment of the costs of maintaining the peg and the private sector's expectations. If private investors expect that the peg might be abandoned, the cost to the government of maintaining a fixed exchange rate becomes higher, and this may indeed lead it to devalue the currency, thus validating market expectations. Obstfeld (1994) provides several examples. One is based on the impact of high government debt. When expectations of an impending devaluation are built into nominal interest rates, maintaining the peg will raise the real debt burden significantly. Under the circumstances, the government might find it too costly to keep the exchange rate unchanged. Conversely, if no devaluation is expected, the cost for the government of maintaining the peg is reduced and the peg will be maintained (see also Bensaid and Jeanne, 1997).[39]

It is important to underscore that the possibility that crises can be self-fulfilling does not imply that the likelihood of an attack is unrelated to fundamentals. Indeed, in second-generation models, there is typically a range of "strong" fundamentals in which a speculative attack would not occur, that is, the government would never find it advantageous to validate market expectations and devalue the currency. Under these circumstances, it would indeed not be rational for market participants to expect a depreciation. Similarly, there is a range of "weak" fundamentals where the cost of defending the peg (the temptation to devalue) is so high that a speculative attack forcing the abandonment of a peg is inevitable. Finally, there is

an intermediate "vulnerable" range of fundamentals, in which a peg could survive if expectations were favorable but would be abandoned if an attack were to materialize (Obstfeld, 1996). A shortcoming of these models is that they do not explain what reasons determine whether the attack takes place or the peg is maintained (see the discussion in Masson, 1998).

Second-generation models suggest that crises may be inherently difficult to predict because the currency attacks may or may not materialize rather than being the inevitable and predictable outcome of a progressive deterioration in fundamentals. Yet, although these models and the various country experiences suggest a number of additional indicators of vulnerability to a currency crisis, they do not differ sharply from those suggested by first-generation models. Both kinds of models of speculative attacks have a similar implication: attacks always occur in countries with weak (or "vulnerable") fundamentals in the macroeconomic sense. In fact, it is usually hard to distinguish whether fundamental policy inconsistencies or self-fulfilling attacks provide the best explanation for a certain episode.[40]

Role of Asset Markets

The models reviewed so far focus squarely on macroeconomic policy. A peg can be abandoned either because of a policy inconsistency or because of a government policy decision that weighs costs and benefits of maintaining the peg. However, some aspects of the Mexican crisis and, especially, the more recent crises in several Asian countries seem to be related to market failures in asset markets or distortions in the financial system, rather than resulting from clear macroeconomic imbalances or an exchange rate misalignment. In all of these episodes, investors refused to roll over short-term debt (Tesobonos in the case of Mexico) and redeemed the proceeds in foreign currency. Authors such as Calvo (1997) have stressed taking a broader view of asset markets rather than focusing exclusively on the evolution of international reserves. For example, if the government is running an unsustainable deficit but resorts to bond financing rather than monetization of the deficit, international reserves may be stable, rather than declining, in the period leading to an attack. The speculative attack essentially occurs in bond markets, as agents refuse to roll over short-term government paper and convert the proceeds into foreign currency.

Although the linkage between financial sector problems and balance of payments crises received prominent attention only after the Mexican crisis in

---

[39]See Calvo (1988) for an earlier application of this idea to the problem of the persistence of high inflation rates.

[40]See Jeanne (1997) for an attempt to detect the effect of self-fulfilling expectations.

1994 and, especially, after the Asian crisis, it had played an important role in previous episodes (see Diaz-Alejandro (1985) for an insightful discussion). For example, the 1982 crisis in Chile was preceded by a period during which the conduct of fiscal policy was conservative, but the private sector borrowed extensively on international markets. The presence of explicit and implicit government guarantees created a severe moral hazard problem, and external shocks precipitated a crisis that resulted in a costly bailout of the banking system and a "socialization" of private external liabilities. With this experience in mind, Velasco (1987) presents a model of currency and banking crises where a negative external shock reduces the value of banks' assets, but because of the deposit guarantee banks do not liquidate bad loans, relying instead on external borrowing to cover their losses. Once access to external borrowing is curtailed, the government has to intervene and bail out the banks. The costs of the bailout and the "socialization" of banks' external liabilities leads to a depletion of foreign exchange reserves and a collapse of the peg. More generally, in situations in which the banking system is fragile because of maturity or currency mismatches, crises can occur because the role of the central bank as lender of last resort comes into conflict with the need to defend the exchange rate peg.

In the Chilean crisis of 1982, self-fulfilling expectations played no role as the crisis was essentially inevitable given the deposit guarantee scheme and the banks' behavior. In contrast, Goldfajn and Valdés (1997) and Chang and Velasco (1998) highlight the role of banking fragility in making a country more vulnerable to speculative attacks. Bank runs based on self-fulfilling expectations can cause the collapse of a solvent but illiquid domestic banking system, as foreign investors refuse to extend credit or roll over existing loans, in a framework similar to that of the well-known banking model of Diamond and Dybvig (1983). Even such purely speculative financial crises can generate large output costs, because banks may be forced to liquidate potentially profitable but illiquid long-term assets to face a liquidity squeeze. A number of factors can make an economy more vulnerable to this type of "run," among them, a large share of short-term external debt and a lowering of reserve requirements. Empirical evidence presented by Kaminsky and Reinhart (1999) indeed shows that banking crises tend to precede balance of payments crises.[41]

In addition to underlining the importance of asset market problems, the recent Asian crisis has drawn attention to the moral hazard generated by implicit government guarantees of private sector external liabilities. In Krugman (1998), government provision of (implicit) bailout guarantees leads to private sector overinvestment and asset price inflation.[42] If the bailout guarantee is not unlimited, asset prices will eventually collapse as the bubble bursts.[43] Corsetti, Pesenti, and Roubini (1998) tell a similar story. In their model, the existence of (implicit or explicit) government guarantees leads firms to "overborrow" from abroad. The guarantees, however, are not unlimited. Under these circumstances, it can be shown that a period of overborrowing can be followed by a sudden withdrawal of external funds once doubts surface over the ability or willingness of the government to cover existing losses. These interpretations of crises do not necessarily emphasize self-fulfilling expectations—rather, they rely on the existence of a fundamental distortion that leads to a gradual buildup of imbalances. One interesting aspect is that the contingent nature of these government liabilities implies that fiscal imbalances will emerge expost, but may not be detectable ex ante.[44]

Recent experience has also focused attention on distortions generating large capital inflows and their later reversal. A model by Dooley (1997) postulates that governments provide insurance against external shocks to the private sector, which is thus enticed to borrow at above-market rates.[45] This attracts capital to the country. However, the available resources of foreign exchange reserves for paying "insurance claims" are limited. This implies that the degree of insurance is declining over time, and therefore the rates of interest that the private sector can afford to pay must also be declining, making the reversal of capital flows eventually unavoidable. When foreigners withdraw their funds, the government steps in to

---

[41]See also Demirgüç-Kunt and Detragiache (1998).

[42]Domestic financial intermediaries will base their decisions on "Panglossian values" for rates of return (i.e., rates of returns that are based only on favorable circumstances, given the government guarantee that would come into effect should circumstances prove unfavorable).

[43]Note that even in this setting in which a crisis is inevitable, self-fulfilling expectations can accelerate the collapse. The reason is that the size of the bailout depends on the magnitude of the fall in asset prices. While government resources may be sufficient to undertake a full bailout for given expectations about asset prices (which would imply no crisis yet) they may be insufficient if asset prices collapse. If agents expect this to occur, they will precipitate a crisis.

[44]It should also be noted that the bursting of an asset price bubble can simply imply that asset prices revert to their fundamental values. In contrast, in models emphasizing lack of liquidity, such as Chang and Velasco (1998), potentially viable projects are liquidated and asset prices can fall below their fundamental value, emphasizing the importance of providing liquidity.

[45]In other words, the existence of insurance is equivalent to an implicit transfer from the government. Some of the proceeds from this transfer are appropriated by domestic financial intermediaries and the rest by foreign lenders, who earn above-market rates on implicitly guaranteed assets.

bail out the private sector, but in so doing it depletes its foreign exchange reserves and a crisis occurs. Dooley underlines that if one includes in the government's "war chest" funds made available by international organizations then the moral hazard problem that leads to the capital inflow-crisis sequence is worsened. He also notes that the model provides a simple explanation for contagion: namely, a large bailout by, say, the IMF or the international community may reduce the resources available for similar bailouts in other developing countries.

Role of Contagion

A feature shared by all the major financial crises of the 1990s—the EMS, the Mexican peso and its tequila effects, Asian currencies, and the Russian ruble—is the spreading of difficulties from one country to another, generally referred to as "contagion." In practice, many factors can account for this phenomenon. First, a crisis in one country may be triggered by a large shock common to several countries—for example, an increase in interest rates on world markets—in which case the crisis can be expected to affect other countries particularly vulnerable to this type of shock.[46] Second, devaluation by one country can affect other countries through "spillover effects." These can occur through several channels. For example, countries that either trade intensively with the country in question or compete with it in third markets will experience a loss in competitiveness and a fall in external demand.[47] The recent crises in East Asia and Russia also highlighted the importance of spillover effects that work through the capital account. For example, the Russian crisis affected the profitability and risk appetite of hedge funds, banks, and other investors, leading to portfolio adjustments that spread difficulties to other markets.[48] Russia's crisis may have led to a revision in expectations concerning the possibility that the IMF would act as a lender of last resort.

Contagion effects proper, in Masson's (1998) taxonomy, occur when crises spread even in the absence of changes in macroeconomic fundamentals. This may occur because of incomplete information and herd behavior on the part of private investors so that a small shock may trigger a massive outflow of capital from several emerging market countries. For example, Calvo and Mendoza (1997) present a model in which investment fund managers choose to "follow the herd" if they are evaluated based on their relative performance vis-à-vis other managers.[49] This type of "collective action" problem increases the likelihood of large swings in capital flows even in the absence of correspondingly large changes in fundamentals. A crisis can also act as a "wake-up call." For example, Goldstein (1998) argues that after the Thai crisis investors reassessed the economic and financial situation of other countries in the region and found them to be less creditworthy than previously believed.

Empirical work on contagion is still at a preliminary stage. The most basic contagion studies assess whether the existence of speculative attacks elsewhere in the world increase the probability of a currency crisis, controlling for a country's macroeconomic, financial, and external sector factors. Studies use either a simple zero/one variable indicating whether there was a crisis elsewhere in the world, or a measure of the number of recent crises in other countries that gives more weight to the most recent crises (see Eichengreen and others, 1996b) and J.P. Morgan, 1998). There is also some evidence that contagion may have a regional dimension (Krueger and others, 1998). However, this finding may be due to the fact that countries within a region often have strong trade ties. In fact, some studies suggest that trade linkages are an important factor of contagion: countries that have strong trade links or compete in an export market with a country experiencing a crisis are themselves more likely to have a crisis (see Eichengreen and others, 1996b and Glick and Rose, 1998). For some episodes, however, it seems difficult to argue that trade links were the only, or even an important, channel of transmission (for example, the pressure on Brazil following the collapse of the Russian ruble in August 1998). Partly for this reason, some analysts have focused on similarities across countries in macroeconomic policies and conditions. However, the hypothesis that contagion spreads more easily to countries with similar macroeconomic fundamentals has not found much empirical support. Testing more directly the importance of financial market spillovers is inherently more difficult, because it would, inter alia, require information on the positions of financial institutions on a global scale.

---

[46]Masson (1998) refers to the effects of type of shock as "monsoonal effects."

[47]Gerlach and Smets (1995) provide a theoretical illustration of this channel and an application to Sweden and Finland.

[48]Valdés (1996) highlights how lack of liquidity in one market hit by a crisis may cause contagion by leading financial intermediaries to liquidate positions in other emerging markets.

[49]Their idea is similar to the one in Scharfstein and Stein (1990), who show that "bad" portfolio managers would mimic the behavior of others so as to "hide in the herd." Calvo and Mendoza also highlight how investors may react to rumors about future returns in a country by shifting their resources out of a country instead of trying to ascertain (at a cost) whether the rumors are founded. If emerging market securities represent a small share of their portfolios, investors would choose not to spend resources trying to ascertain whether the rumor is accurate.

References

Adams, Charles, Donald J. Mathieson, Garry Schinasi, and Bankim Chadha, 1998, *International Capital Markets, September 1998: A Survey by the Staff of the International Monetary Fund*, World Economic and Financial Surveys (Washington: International Monetary Fund).

Agénor, Pierre-Richard, Jagdeep S. Bhandari, and Robert P. Flood, 1992, "Speculative Attacks and Models of Balance of Payments Crises," *Staff Papers*, International Monetary Fund, Vol. 39 (June), pp. 357–94.

Agénor, Pierre-Richard, and Paul Masson, 1999, "Credibility, Reputation, and the Mexican Peso Crisis," *Journal of Money, Credit and Banking*, No. 1 (February), pp. 70–84.

Banerjee, Abhijit, V., 1992, "A Simple Model of Herd Behavior," *Quarterly Journal of Economics*, Vol. 107 (August), pp. 797–817.

Bartolini, Leonardo, and Allan Drazen, 1997, "Capital Account Liberalization as a Signal," *American Economic Review*, Vol. 87 (March), pp. 138–54.

Bensaid, Bernard, and Olivier Jeanne, 1997, "The Instability of Fixed Exchange Rate Systems When Raising the Nominal Interest Rate Is Costly," *European Economic Review*, Vol. 41 (August), pp. 1461–78.

Berg, Andrew, 1999, "The Asia Crisis: Causes, Policy Responses, and Outcomes," IMF Working Paper No. 99/138 (Washington: International Monetary Fund).

Berg, Andrew, and Catherine Pattillo, 1999a, "Are Currency Crises Predictable? A Test," *IMF Staff Papers*, Vol. 46 (June), pp. 107–38.

———, 1999b "Predicting Currency Crises: The Indicators Approach and an Alternative," *Journal of International Money and Finance*, Vol. 18, pp. 561–86.

Bikhchandani, Sushil, David Hirshleifer, and Ivo Welch, 1992, "A Theory of Fads, Custom and Cultural Change as Informational Cascades," *Journal of Political Economy*, Vol. 100, pp. 992–1026.

Blanco, Herminio, and Peter Garber, 1986, "Recurrent Devaluation and Speculative Attacks on the Mexican Peso," *Journal of Political Economy*, Vol. 94 (February), pp. 148–66.

Buiter, Willem H., Giancarlo Corsetti, and Paolo A. Pesenti, 1998, *Interpreting the ERM Crisis: Country-Specific and Systemic Issues*, Princeton Studies in International Finance No. 84 (Princeton, New Jersey: Princeton University Press).

Calvo, Guillermo, 1987, "Balance of Payments Crises in a Cash-in-Advance Economy," *Journal of Money, Credit and Banking*, Vol. 19 (February), pp. 19–32.

———, 1988, "Servicing the Public Debt: The Role of Expectations," *American Economic Review*, Vol. 78 (September), pp. 647–71.

———, 1997, "Varieties of Capital Market Crises," in *The Debt Burden and Its Consequences for Monetary Policy*, ed. by Guillermo Calvo and Mervyn King (New York: St. Martin's Press).

Calvo, Guillermo, and Enrique Mendoza, 1996, "Mexico's Balance of Payments Crisis: A Chronicle of a Death Foretold," *Journal of International Economics*, Vol. 41 (November), pp. 235–64.

———, 1997, "Rational Herd Behavior and the Globalization of Securities' Markets" (unpublished; College Park, Maryland: University of Maryland).

Chang, Roberto, and Andrés Velasco, 1998, "Financial Crises in Emerging Markets: A Canonical Model," NBER Working Paper No. 6606 (Cambridge, Massachusetts: National Bureau of Economic Research).

Chari, V. V., and Harold Cole, 1997, "Hot Money," NBER Working Paper No. 6007 (Cambridge, Massachusetts: National Bureau of Economic Research).

Citicorp Securities Inc., 1998, *Early Warning System—Anticipating Balance-of-Payments Crises in Latin America*, May 6, 1998 (New York).

Cline, William, 1995, *International Debt Reexamined* (Washington: Institute for International Economics).

Cole, Harold I., and Timothy J. Kehoe, 1996, "A Self-Fulfilling Model of Mexico's 1994–1995 Debt Crisis," *Journal of International Economics*, Vol. 41 (November), pp. 309–30.

Connolly, Michael B., 1986, "The Speculative Attack on the Peso and the Real Exchange Rate: Argentina 1979–81," *Journal of International Money and Finance*, Vol. 5 (March), pp. S117–S130.

Cooper, Richard, N., 1971, *Currency Devaluation in Developing Countries*, Princeton Essays in International Finance No. 86 (Princeton, New Jersey: Princeton University Press).

Corsetti, Giancarlo, Paolo Pesenti, and Nouriel Roubini, 1998, "Paper Tigers? A Preliminary Assessment of the Asian Crisis" (unpublished; Lisbon: NBER-Bank of Portugal International Seminar, June).

Credit Suisse First Boston, 1998, *Emerging Markets Risk Indicator*, Technical Report (London).

Cumby, Robert, E., and Sweder van Wijnbergen, 1989, "Financial Policy and Speculative Runs with a Crawling Peg: Argentina 1979–1981," *Journal of International Economics*, Vol. 27 (August), pp. 111–27.

Dellas, Harris, and Alan Stockman, 1993, "Self-Fulfilling Expectations, Speculative Attacks, and Capital Controls," *Journal of Money, Credit and Banking*, Vol. 25 (November), pp. 721–30.

Demirgüç-Kunt, Asli, and Enrica Detragiache, 1998, "Financial Liberalization and Financial Fragility," IMF Working Paper No. 98/83 (Washington: International Monetary Fund).

Diamond, Douglas W., and Philip H. Dybvig, 1983, "Bank Runs, Deposit Insurance and Liquidity," *Journal of Political Economy*, Vol. 91 (June), pp. 401–19.

Diaz-Alejandro, Carlos, 1985, "Goodbye Financial Repression, Hello Financial Crash," *Journal of Development Economics*, Vol. 19 (September–October), pp. 1–24.

Dooley, Michael P., 1997, "A Model of Crises in Emerging Markets," NBER Working Paper No. 6300 (Cambridge, Massachusetts: National Bureau of Economic Research).

Dornbusch, Rudiger, Ilan Goldfajn, and Rodrigo O. Valdés, 1995, "Currency Crises and Collapses," *Brookings Papers on Economic Activity: 2,* Brookings Institution, pp. 219–93.

Drazen, Allan, 1999, "Political Contagion in Currency Crises," NBER Working Paper No. 7211 (Cambridge, Massachusetts: National Bureau of Economic Research).

———, and Paul Masson, 1994, "Credibility of Policy Versus Credibility of Policymakers," *Quarterly Journal of Economics*, Vol. 109 (August), pp. 735–54.

Edwards, Sebastian, 1989, *Real Exchange Rates, Devaluation and Adjustment: Exchange Rate Policy in Developing Countries* (Cambridge, Massachusetts: MIT Press).

———, and Peter J. Montiel, 1989, "Devaluation Crises and the Macroeconomic Consequences of Postponed Adjustment in Developing Countries," *Staff Papers,* International Monetary Fund, Vol. 36 (December), pp. 875–903.

Eichengreen, Barry, and Charles Wyplosz, 1993, "The Unstable EMS," *Brookings Papers on Economic Activity: 1,* Brookings Institution, pp. 51–143.

Eichengreen, Barry, Andrew K. Rose, and Charles Wyplosz, 1995, "Exchange Market Mayhem: The Antecedents and Aftermath of Speculative Attacks," *Economic Policy*, Vol. 21 (October), pp. 249–312.

———, 1996a, "Is There a Safe Passage to EMU? Evidence from Capital Controls and a Proposal," in *The Microstructure of Foreign Exchange Markets*, ed. by Jeffrey A. Frankel, Giampaolo Galli, and Alberto Giovannini (Chicago: University of Chicago Press).

———, 1996b, "Contagious Currency Crises," CEPR Working Paper No. 1453 (London: Centre for Economic Policy Research).

Esquivel, Gerardo, and Felipe Larraín, 1998, "Explaining Currency Crises," Development Discussion Paper No. 666 (Cambridge, Massachusetts: Harvard Institute for International Development).

Flood, Robert, and Peter Garber, 1984a, "Collapsing Exchange Rate Regimes: Some Linear Examples," *Journal of International Economics*, Vol. 17 (August), pp. 1–14.

———, 1984b, "Gold Monetization and Gold Discipline," *Journal of Political Economy*, Vol. 92 (February), pp. 90–107.

Flood, Robert, and Nancy Marion, 1998a, "Perspectives on the Recent Currency Crises Literature," NBER Working Paper No. 6380 (Cambridge, Massachusetts: National Bureau of Economic Research).

———, 1998b, "Self-Fulfilling Risk Predictions: An Application to Speculative Attacks," IMF Working Paper No. 98/124 (Washington: International Monetary Fund).

Frankel, Jeffrey, and Andrew Rose, 1996, "Currency Crashes in Emerging Markets: An Empirical Treatment," *Journal of International Economics*, Vol. 41 (November), pp. 351–66.

Garber, Peter, and Lars E. O. Svensson, 1995, "The Operation and Collapse of Fixed Exchange Rate Regimes," in *Handbook of International Economics*, Vol. 3, ed. by Gene M. Grossman and Kenneth Rogoff (Amsterdam: North-Holland).

Gerlach, Stefan, and Frank Smets, 1995, "Contagious Speculative Attacks," *European Journal of Political Economy*, Vol. 11 (March), pp. 45–63.

Glick, Reuven, and Andrew K. Rose, 1998, "Contagion and Trade: Why Are Currency Crises Regional?" CEPR Discussion Paper No. 1947 (London: Centre for Economic Policy Research).

Goldberg, Linda, 1994, "Predicting Exchange Rate Crises: Mexico Revisited," *Journal of International Economics*, Vol. 36 (May), pp. 413–30.

Goldfajn, Ilan, and Rodrigo Valdés, 1997, "Capital Flows and Twin Crises: The Role of Liquidity," IMF Working Paper 97/87 (Washington: International Monetary Fund).

———, 1998, "Are Currency Crises Predictable?" *European Economic Review*, Vol. 42 (May), pp. 873–85.

———, 1999, "The Aftermath of Appreciations," *Quarterly Journal of Economics,* Vol. 114 (February), pp. 229–62.

Goldman Sachs, 1998, *GS-Watch: A New Framework for Predicting Financial Crises in Emerging Markets*, by Alberto Ades, Rumi Masih, and Daniel Tenengauzer, December 18, 1998.

Goldstein, Morris, 1998, "Early Warning Indicators and the Asian Financial Crisis" (unpublished; Washington: Institute for International Economics).

International Monetary Fund, 1998, *World Economic Outlook, May 1998: A Survey by the Staff of the International Monetary Fund*, World Economic and Financial Surveys (Washington).

Jeanne, Olivier, 1996, "Would a Tobin Tax Have Saved the EMS?" *Scandinavian Journal of Economics*, Vol. 98, pp. 503–20.

———, 1997, "Are Currency Crises Self-Fulfilling? A Test," *Journal of International Economics*, Vol. 43 (November), pp. 263–86.

J. P. Morgan, 1998, *Event Risk Indicator Handbook*, January 29 (London).

Kaminsky, Graciela, 1998, "Currency and Banking Crises: The Early Warnings of Distress," International Finance Discussion Paper No. 629 (Washington: Board of Governors of the Federal Reserve System).

———, Saúl Lizondo, and Carmen M. Reinhart, 1998, "Leading Indicators of Currency Crises," *Staff Papers*, International Monetary Fund, Vol. 45 (March) pp. 1–48.

Kaminsky, Graciela, and Carmen M. Reinhart, 1999, "The Twin Crises: The Causes of Banking and Balance-of-Payments Problems," *American Economic Review*, Vol. 89 (June), pp. 473–500.

Kochhar, Kalpana, Prakash Loungani, and Mark R. Stone, 1998, "The East Asian Crisis: Macroeconomic Developments and Policy Lessons," IMF Working Paper No. 98/128 (Washington: International Monetary Fund).

Krasker, William S., 1980, "The 'Peso Problem' in Testing the Efficiency of Forward Exchange Markets," *Journal of Monetary Economics*, Vol. 6 (April), pp. 269–76.

Krueger, Mark, Patrick N. Osakwe, and Jennifer Page, 1998, "Fundamentals, Contagion and Currency Crises: An Empirical Analysis," Bank of Canada Working Paper 98-10 (Ottawa: Bank of Canada).

Krugman, Paul, 1979, "A Model of Balance-of-Payments Crises," *Journal of Money, Credit and Banking*, Vol. 11 (August), pp. 311–25.

———, 1996, "Are Currency Crises Self-Fulfilling?" *NBER Macroeconomics Annual* (Cambridge, Massachusetts: National Bureau of Economic Research).

———, 1998, "Bubble, Boom, Crash: Theoretical Notes on Asia's Crisis" (unpublished; Cambridge, Massachusetts: Massachusetts Institute of Technology).

Kumar, Manmohan, Uma Moorthy, and William Perraudin, 1998, "Predicting Emerging Market Currency Crises," CEPR Discussion Paper No. (London: Centre for Economic Policy Research).

Lehman Brothers, 1998, *Emerging Markets Strategy*, May 15, 1998.

Masson, Paul, 1998, "Contagion: Monsoonal Effects, Spillovers, and Jumps Between Multiple Equilibria," IMF Working Paper No. 98/142 (Washington: International Monetary Fund).

Milesi-Ferretti, Gian Maria, and Assaf Razin, 1998, "Current Account Reversals and Currency Crises: Empirical Regularities," IMF Working Paper No. 98/89 (Washington: International Monetary Fund).

Moreno, Ramon, 1995, "Macroeconomic Behavior During Periods of Speculative Pressure or Realignment: Evidence from Pacific Basin Economies," *Economic Review*, Federal Reserve Bank of San Francisco, No. 3, pp. 3–16.

Obstfeld, Maurice, 1986, "Rational and Self-Fulfilling Balance of Payments Crises," *American Economic Review*, Vol. 76 (March), pp. 72–81.

———, 1994, "The Logic of Currency Crises," *Cahiers Economiques et Monétaires*, Vol. 43, pp. 189–213.

———, 1996, "Models of Crises with Self-Fulfilling Features," *European Economic Review*, Vol. 40 (April), pp. 1037–47.

Obstfeld, Maurice, and Kenneth Rogoff, 1995, "The Mirage of Fixed Exchange Rates," *Journal of Economic Perspectives*, Vol. 9 (Fall), pp. 73–96.

Ozkan, F. Gulcin, and Alan Sutherland, 1995, "Policy Measures to Avoid a Currency Crisis," *Economic Journal*, Vol. 105 (March), pp. 510–19.

———, 1998, "A Currency Crisis Model with an Optimising Policymaker," *Journal of International Economics*, Vol. 44 (April), pp. 339–64.

Penati, Alessandro, and George Pennacchi, 1989, "Optimal Portfolio Choice and the Collapse of a Fixed-Exchange Rate Regime," *Journal of International Economics*, Vol. 27 (August), pp. 1–24.

Radelet, Steven, and Jeffrey Sachs, 1998a, "The Onset of the East Asian Financial Crisis," NBER Working Paper No. 6680 (Cambridge, Massachusetts: National Bureau of Economic Research).

———, 1998b, "The East Asian Financial Crisis: Diagnosis, Remedies, Prospects," *Brookings Papers on Economic Activity: 1*, Brookings Institution, pp. 1–90.

Sachs, Jeffrey, Aaron Tornell, and Andrés Velasco, 1996a, "Financial Crises in Emerging Markets: The Lessons from 1995," *Brookings Papers on Economic Activity: 1*, Brookings Institution, pp. 147–215.

———, 1996b, "The Collapse of the Mexican Peso: What Have We Learned?" *Economic Policy*, Vol. 22 (April), pp. 15–63.

Salant, Stephen W., and Dale W. Henderson, 1978, "Market Anticipations of Government Policies and the Price of Gold," *Journal of Political Economy*, Vol. 86 (August), pp. 627–48.

Savastano, Miguel, 1992, "Collapse of a Crawling Peg Regime in the Presence of a Government Budget Constraint," *Staff Papers*, International Monetary Fund, Vol. 39 (March), pp. 79–100.

Scharfstein, David, and Jerome Stein, 1990, "Herd Behavior and Investment," *American Economic Review*, Vol. 80 (June), pp. 465–79.

Summers, Lawrence, 1995, "Ten Lessons to Learn," *The Economist*, December 23, pp. 46–48.

Tornell, Aaron, 1998, "Common Fundamentals in the Tequila and Asian Crises" (unpublished; Cambridge, Massachusetts: Harvard University).

Valdés, Rodrigo, 1996, "Emerging Market Contagion: Evidence and Theory" (unpublished).

Velasco, Andrés, 1987, "Financial Crises and Balance of Payments Crises: A Simple Model of the Southern Cone Experience," *Journal of Development Economics*, Vol. 27 (October), pp. 263–83.

Werner, Alejandro, 1996, "Mexico's Currency Risk Premia in 1992–94: A Closer Look at the Interest Rate Differentials," IMF Working Paper No. 96/41 (Washington: International Monetary Fund).

Recent Occasional Papers of the International Monetary Fund

186. Anticipating Balance of Payments Crises: The Role of Early Warning Systems, by Andrew Berg, Eduardo Borensztein, Gian Maria Milesi-Ferretti, and Catherine Pattillo. 1999.

185. Oman Beyond the Oil Horizon: Policies Toward Sustainable Growth, edited by Ahsan Mansur and Volker Treichel. 1999.

184. Growth Experience in Transition Countries, 1990–98, by Oleh Havrylyshyn, Thomas Wolf, Julian Berengaut, Marta Castello-Branco, Ron van Rooden, and Valerie Mercer-Blackman. 1999.

183. Economic Reforms in Kazakhstan, Kyrgyz Republic, Tajikistan, Turkmenistan, and Uzbekistan, by Emine Gürgen, Harry Snoek, Jon Craig, Jimmy McHugh, Ivailo Izvorski, and Ron van Rooden. 1999.

182. Tax Reform in the Baltics, Russia, and Other Countries of the Former Soviet Union, by a Staff Team Led by Liam Ebrill and Oleh Havrylyshyn. 1999.

181. The Netherlands: Transforming a Market Economy, by C. Maxwell Watson, Bas B. Bakker, Jan Kees Martijn, and Ioannis Halikias. 1999.

180. Revenue Implications of Trade Liberalization, by Liam Ebrill, Janet Stotsky, and Reint Gropp. 1999.

179. Dinsinflation in Transition: 1993–97, by Carlo Cottarelli and Peter Doyle. 1999.

178. IMF-Supported Programs in Indonesia, Korea, and Thailand: A Preliminary Assessment, by Timothy Lane, Atish Ghosh, Javier Hamann, Steven Phillips, Marianne Schulze-Ghattas, and Tsidi Tsikata. 1999.

177. Perspectives on Regional Unemployment in Europe, by Paolo Mauro, Esawar Prasad, and Antonio Spilimbergo. 1999.

176. Back to the Future: Postwar Reconstruction and Stabilization in Lebanon, edited by Sena Eken and Thomas Helbling. 1999.

175. Macroeconomic Developments in the Baltics, Russia, and Other Countries of the Former Soviet Union, 1992–97, by Luis M. Valdivieso. 1998.

174. Impact of EMU on Selected Non–European Union Countries, by R. Feldman, K. Nashashibi, R. Nord, P. Allum, D. Desruelle, K. Enders, R. Kahn, and H. Temprano-Arroyo. 1998.

173. The Baltic Countries: From Economic Stabilization to EU Accession, by Julian Berengaut, Augusto Lopez-Claros, Françoise Le Gall, Dennis Jones, Richard Stern, Ann-Margret Westin, Effie Psalida, Pietro Garibaldi. 1998.

172. Capital Account Liberalization: Theoretical and Practical Aspects, by a staff team led by Barry Eichengreen and Michael Mussa, with Giovanni Dell'Ariccia, Enrica Detragiache, Gian Maria Milesi-Ferretti, and Andrew Tweedie. 1998.

171. Monetary Policy in Dollarized Economies, by Tomás Baliño, Adam Bennett, and Eduardo Borensztein. 1998.

170. The West African Economic and Monetary Union: Recent Developments and Policy Issues, by a staff team led by Ernesto Hernández-Catá and comprising Christian A. François, Paul Masson, Pascal Bouvier, Patrick Peroz, Dominique Desruelle, and Athanasios Vamvakidis. 1998.

169. Financial Sector Development in Sub-Saharan African Countries, by Hassanali Mehran, Piero Ugolini, Jean Phillipe Briffaux, George Iden, Tonny Lybek, Stephen Swaray, and Peter Hayward. 1998.

168. Exit Strategies: Policy Options for Countries Seeking Greater Exchange Rate Flexibility, by a staff team led by Barry Eichengreen and Paul Masson with Hugh Bredenkamp, Barry Johnston, Javier Hamann, Esteban Jadresic, and Inci Ötker. 1998.

167. Exchange Rate Assessment: Extensions of the Macroeconomic Balance Approach, edited by Peter Isard and Hamid Faruqee. 1998

166. Hedge Funds and Financial Market Dynamics, by a staff team led by Barry Eichengreen and Donald Mathieson with Bankim Chadha, Anne Jansen, Laura Kodres, and Sunil Sharma. 1998.

165. Algeria: Stabilization and Transition to the Market, by Karim Nashashibi, Patricia Alonso-Gamo, Stefania Bazzoni, Alain Féler, Nicole Laframboise, and Sebastian Paris Horvitz. 1998.

164. MULTIMOD Mark III: The Core Dynamic and Steady-State Model, by Douglas Laxton, Peter Isard, Hamid Faruqee, Eswar Prasad, and Bart Turtelboom. 1998.

163. Egypt: Beyond Stabilization, Toward a Dynamic Market Economy, by a staff team led by Howard Handy. 1998.

162. Fiscal Policy Rules, by George Kopits and Steven Symansky. 1998.

161. The Nordic Banking Crises: Pitfalls in Financial Liberalization? by Burkhard Dress and Ceyla Pazarbaşıoğlu. 1998.

160. Fiscal Reform in Low-Income Countries: Experience Under IMF-Supported Programs, by a staff team led by George T. Abed and comprising Liam Ebrill, Sanjeev Gupta, Benedict Clements, Ronald Mc-Morran, Anthony Pellechio, Jerald Schiff, and Marijn Verhoeven. 1998.

159. Hungary: Economic Policies for Sustainable Growth, Carlo Cottarelli, Thomas Krueger, Reza Moghadam, Perry Perone, Edgardo Ruggiero, and Rachel van Elkan. 1998.

158. Transparency in Government Operations, by George Kopits and Jon Craig. 1998.

157. Central Bank Reforms in the Baltics, Russia, and the Other Countries of the Former Soviet Union, by a staff team led by Malcolm Knight and comprising Susana Almuiña, John Dalton, Inci Otker, Ceyla Pazarbaşıoğlu, Arne B. Petersen, Peter Quirk, Nicholas M. Roberts, Gabriel Sensenbrenner, and Jan Willem van der Vossen. 1997.

156. The ESAF at Ten Years: Economic Adjustment and Reform in Low-Income Countries, by the staff of the International Monetary Fund. 1997.

155. Fiscal Policy Issues During the Transition in Russia, by Augusto Lopez-Claros and Sergei V. Alexashenko. 1998.

154. Credibility Without Rules? Monetary Frameworks in the Post–Bretton Woods Era, by Carlo Cottarelli and Curzio Giannini. 1997.

153. Pension Regimes and Saving, by G.A. Mackenzie, Philip Gerson, and Alfredo Cuevas. 1997.

152. Hong Kong, China: Growth, Structural Change, and Economic Stability During the Transition, by John Dodsworth and Dubravko Mihaljek. 1997.

151. Currency Board Arrangements: Issues and Experiences, by a staff team led by Tomás J.T. Baliño and Charles Enoch. 1997.

150. Kuwait: From Reconstruction to Accumulation for Future Generations, by Nigel Andrew Chalk, Mohamed A. El-Erian, Susan J. Fennell, Alexei P. Kireyev, and John F. Wilson. 1997.

149. The Composition of Fiscal Adjustment and Growth: Lessons from Fiscal Reforms in Eight Economies, by G.A. Mackenzie, David W.H. Orsmond, and Philip R. Gerson. 1997.

148. Nigeria: Experience with Structural Adjustment, by Gary Moser, Scott Rogers, and Reinold van Til, with Robin Kibuka and Inutu Lukonga. 1997.

147. Aging Populations and Public Pension Schemes, by Sheetal K. Chand and Albert Jaeger. 1996.

146. Thailand: The Road to Sustained Growth, by Kalpana Kochhar, Louis Dicks-Mireaux, Balazs Horvath, Mauro Mecagni, Erik Offerdal, and Jianping Zhou. 1996.

145. Exchange Rate Movements and Their Impact on Trade and Investment in the APEC Region, by Takatoshi Ito, Peter Isard, Steven Symansky, and Tamim Bayoumi. 1996.

144. National Bank of Poland: The Road to Indirect Instruments, by Piero Ugolini. 1996.

143. Adjustment for Growth: The African Experience, by Michael T. Hadjimichael, Michael Nowak, Robert Sharer, and Amor Tahari. 1996.

142. Quasi-Fiscal Operations of Public Financial Institutions, by G.A. Mackenzie and Peter Stella. 1996.

Note: For information on the title and availability of Occasional Papers not listed, please consult the IMF Publications Catalog or contact IMF Publication Services.